HOLDOUTS!

The Buildings
That Got In The Way

by
ANDREW ALPERN
and
SEYMOUR DURST

with a Foreword to the Third Edition
by Vishaan Chakrabarti

and a Foreword to the Second Edition
by Norman Marcus

and a Foreword to the First Edition
by John V. Lindsay

OLD YORK FOUNDATION
in association with
DAVID R. GODINE · PUBLISHER

LIBRARY OF CONGRESS CATALOGING-IN-PUBLICATION DATA

Alpern, Andrew.
  [Holdouts!]
 Holdouts! : the buildings that got in the way / by Andrew Alpern and Seymour Durst ; with
a foreword to the third edition by Vishaan Chakrabarti and a foreword to the second edition
by Norman Marcus and a foreword to the first edition by John V. Lindsay. – [3rd ed].
    p. cm.
  Rev. ed. of: New York's architectural holdouts. 1996.
   ISBN-13: 978-1-56792-443-5
   ISBN-10: 1-56792-443-3
  1. Real estate development–New York (State)–New York–Case studies. 2. Real property-
-Valuation–New York (State)–New York–Case studies. 3. Real estate development–Case
 studies. 4. Real property–Valuation–Case studies. I. Durst, Seymour B., 1913-1995
 II. Alpern, Andrew 1938-   . New York's architectural holdouts. III. Title. IV. Title: Buildings
 that got in the way.
   HD268.N5A46 2011
   333.33'8–dc23
                                                                              2011019753

Book design revisions and production by Jerry Kelly

Published by Old York Foundation, in care of The Durst Organization
One Bryant Park, 1111 Sixth Avenue, New York NY 10036
Distributed by
David R. Godine, Publisher
Post Office Box 450, Jaffrey, New Hampshire 03452
www.godine.com

BIBLIOGRAPHIC NOTE: *HOLDOUTS! The Buildings That Got In The Way,* first published by Old York Foundation in
2011, is a slightly altered republication of the work published by Dover Publications Inc. in 1996 under the title *New York's
Architectural Holdouts,* which in turn was a slightly altered republication of the work originally published by McGraw-Hill
Book Company in 1984 under the title *HOLDOUTS!*

Manufactured in the United States

Contents

Foreword
to the Third Edition

by VISHAAN CHAKRABARTI

Published originally in 1984 with a foreword by Mayor John V. Lindsay, and with a subsequent edition in 1996, *HOLDOUTS!* remains fresh, fascinating, and all the more relevant to a planet urbanizing at a lightning pace. More people live in cities than rural areas for the first time in world history, and with the population of the planet projected to increase by approximately fifty percent by mid-century, the United Nations anticipates that the proportion of the planet's population that will live in cities by 2050 may well exceed a staggering seventy-five percent. This intensely increasing rural-to-urban migration will place that much more pressure on the price and desirability of land in center city locations, creating many more holdouts for the foreseeable future.

The now infamous story of the Chinese city of Chongquing's "nail house" (essentially a colloquialism for a holdout or a nail that cannot be taken out or hammered down) illustrates vividly the tensions of a world in the midst of growing pains. The *New York Times*, in a prominently featured story in March 2007, described the land owner Wu Ping as "anything but an ordinary woman" who for years stood up to the government and its development partners to the shock and surprise of the Chinese populace. Ultimately the owner did settle and the site was redeveloped, but the incident sent tremors through China's body politic, and left no doubt as to Mayor Lindsay's observation in his original foreword to this book that, "Finding ways of mediating between competing interests is one of government's most difficult and crucial responsibilities. The tensions between private rights and public purposes continue to affect the lives of every citizen."

In fact, the very notion of public purpose in land acquisition and eminent domain has been called into question. In 2005, the United States Supreme Court held in the case of *Kelo vs. the City of New London*, that the City of New London, Connecticut in condemning Susan Kelo's land for a redevelopment desired by the Pfizer corporation did so justifiably because its "proposed disposition of petitioners' property qualifies as a 'public use' within the meaning of the Takings Clause" of the Fifth Amendment of the Constitution. In a 5-4 decision the Court essentially found that a taking called for under a municipality's comprehensive economic development plan constitutes a public purpose and is therefore constitutional. Interestingly, the four justices who dissented represented the conservative wing of the Court, upending the conventional wisdom that conservatives defend big business while liberals defend the little guy. The politics of eminent domain has made strange bedfellows indeed, with traditionally liberal organizations like the American Civil Liberties Union finding common cause with conservative politicians and libertarians to supplant the Kelo finding with local laws that curb government-sponsored eminent domain. Similarly, New York State's highest court ruled in June 2010 that the private Columbia University's proposed use of a large site in Harlem for its new northern campus constituted a use of the land for a public purpose because of the nature of Columbia's educational activities expected for that site. Because of this, the court determined that the land could be condemned and taken from its private owners (with fair compensation, of course) under the principle of eminent domain.

Throughout *HOLDOUTS!* the reader senses the authors' sensitivities to this tension between private property rights and the overwhelming need in big cities for coherent, large-scale economic development, and they express this sensitivity by giving names and stories to both the power players and the small land and business owners who stand in their way. And this book certainly offers up a generous assortment of characters. You'll meet Joseph Richardson, who in 1882 built an apartment on a five-foot strip of land simply to thwart the ambitions of the neighboring developer who had refused to pay Richardson's holdout price (the construction came to be known as the "Spite House").

1 China's most famous holdout: the Chongqing "Nail House" with a sign reading "The legal private property that belongs to a citizen should not be violated." *(Derek Kolb)*

Then there's Mrs. Robert Bacon, the quintessential "little old lady" holdout whose mid-nineteenth-century cottage remained standing at the northeast corner of 34th Street and Park Avenue until after her death in the 1950s. The descendants of John Jay, the nation's first Supreme Court justice, have kept the little plot at 88 Broad Street in the family for nearly three centuries in honor of the purchase of that land in 1720 by their ancestor and the request by a Jay descendent in his will of 1843 that his son and later heirs hang on to the first piece of land that his great-grandfather Augustus Jay purchased in the New World. The authors seem to find in these figures the kinds of holdout that even a developer can admire.

Nonetheless, there's never any real question where the sympathies of Mr. Durst and Mr. Alpern ultimately lie. In the preface to the first edition, they caution that "the effects of holdouts could be detrimental to more people than just the unfortunate builder," and close with the modest aspiration that their book "may perhaps encourage a public awareness of holdouts that will help prevent interference with the rejuvenation of New York." This book characterizes many holdouts as straightforward impediments to progress. The authors take few pains to conceal their satisfaction when narrating unhappy outcomes for particularly recalcitrant owners whose greed or ignorance obstructed an unambiguous improvement to their neighborhoods. Even Mayor Lindsay, who takes an even-handed approach to the question in his foreword, states that given the extraordinary contribution of large-scale real estate to a city's tax base, that "there is little question that contemporary municipal fiscal, social, and economic pressures all make the construction of office towers and apartment buildings of utmost importance to city dwellers."

In recent memory no holdout story received more attention here in New York than that of Daniel Goldstein and the Atlantic Yards, the massive redevelopment project sponsored by Forest City Ratner in central Brooklyn. The site, originally consisting of rail yards as well as adjacent properties with low-lying residential uses and some small businesses, was reconceived by the State's redevelopment arm and the powerful developer as a home to a new arena and thousands of units of market rate and affordable housing units. Mr. Goldstein, a resident in the adjacent property, refused to sell and decided to fight the project by forming a group entitled Develop Don't Destroy Brooklyn.

After years of litigation, Mr. Goldstein, like Wu Ping, ultimately settled with the development team. For a grand sum of $3 million, about a six-fold increase over his original purchase price, Mr. Goldstein agreed to vacate his family home and stop fighting the project. The redevelopment construction project is now proceeding.

During his long career, real estate developer Seymour Durst encountered more than his share of owners and residents demanding exorbitant sums for their inconvenient buildings. Indeed, some of them appear in the following pages. So on the matter of holdouts, it may be fairly noted that Seymour Durst

2 Daniel Goldstein *(Willens/AP)*

3 Rendering of Atlantic Yards *(SHoP Architects)*

4 A stand-out holdout in Milan, Italy in 2000
(*courtesy of Andrea Costa*)

was by no means a disinterested party. His co-author, Andrew Alpern, was interested in a long held religious tenet "to respect the right of others to do things in a different way from our ways." The authors' diverse backgrounds but convergent beliefs make this book a nuanced, broadminded, and always entertaining view of the phenomenon of holdouts. Mr. Durst could not have found a better partner in this undertaking than Mr. Alpern, a lawyer, an architect, an architectural historian, and a prolific writer. Together, they compiled an exhaustively researched compendium of New York City buildings that have held their ground as the surrounding blocks evolved, and of those individuals who have for better or worse exerted disproportionate influence in shaping the City's architectural landscape.

Some of the holdouts you will read about have since given way to developments that now seem inevitable. Many of the Park Avenue pariahs Mr. Durst and Mr. Alpern find so objectionable are now luxury apartments. H.P. Kraus's rare book dealership at 16 East 46th Street, which eventually became the final address of the Gotham Book Mart, has been razed to make room for a high-priced boutique hotel. Likewise, the "seedy-looking relic" at 679 Third Avenue that prevented the Durst Organization from continuing an assemblage the full length of the block has been replaced with a sleek glass retail space more consistent with the Durst building's architecture, at last resolving the "visual cacophony" the authors lament.

But many more of the buildings detailed in this volume remain to this day. You can still find the one-story hut at 1129 Broadway squatting between the towering Townsend and St. James Buildings, and now housing a garment wholesaler. At 592 Eighth Avenue stands the much altered and now unrecognizable sole remaining unit of a row of modest three-story brick-fronted houses built in the 1850s offering dwellings for citizens seeking a safe distance from the heart of town during a resurgence of yellow fever. On Broadway and 97th, you will see the long narrow two-story building that once bordered a beer garden owned and operated by Adolphus Busch, until Prohibition closed the gates on that venture. For the enthusiastic reader, *HOLDOUTS!* can function as a kind of field guide.

Like every great book about architecture and urbanism, *HOLDOUTS!* will change the way you walk around New York, or any city around the world in which real estate is at a premium and the old must make room for new. The next time you spot a three-story brick façade wedged between two looming modern office towers, the next time you see a corner cut out of an extravagant structure that might otherwise command an entire city block, you will recognize a likely holdout. You may find yourself wondering about the people behind these real estate clashes that have left their mark on the cityscape. What drove the individual owners and would-be developers to loggerheads over that particular parcel of land? And wherever your sympathies ultimately lie, wherever you live or work, your perspective will be richer for having read this book.

Foreword
to the Second Edition
by NORMAN MARCUS

The original edition of this book was written in the early 1980s, a commercial real-estate development boom decade. The authors anticipated a renewal of the pressures that had created holdouts in the past, but for many reasons this did not occur.

It may be useful to point out why.

What is a holdout? Typically, it is the person who owns or has a lease on a small parcel of land, frequently with an occupied older building, that stands athwart an otherwise cleared assemblage, ready for new construction but for the holdout. To make way for the development, the owner demands many times the value of his modest parcel. To the untutored eye, a sleek, modern, high-rise office building juxtaposed with a nondescript example of holdout schlock is not a pretty picture. It might even reduce rents in the new structure unless eliminated.

Holdouts attained much of their power as a by-product of central-business-district zoning regulations that favored, and occasionally required, large-lot development. Building coverage of the land typically was restricted to 25 or 40 percent of the lot, with a 20 percent bonus in total floor area in the building in exchange for a publicly accessible plaza on the uncovered portion of the site. The larger the lot, the larger the tower. Small, strategically located holdout lots gained much leverage in the zoning-induced hunt for large midtown lots eligible for maximum development.

The city changed these regulations in the 1980s. The public had grown fearful of widespread drug dealing in public plazas and preferred less overbearing buildings—buildings that were aligned along the sidewalk and touched their neighbors. The plaza bonus was cut to one-third of its previous value and the small-lot ziggurat buildings with fuller coverage and receding setbacks at the top, such as were common in the 1920s, began to be built again.

On a different track, by 1990 two percent of all city buildings were either designated landmarks or located in historic districts, subject to development restrictions imposed by the New York City Landmarks Preservation Commission. Holdout scenarios generated by intense assemblage activity were preempted by landmark or historic-district designations. When a developer was confronted with these buildings, the romance of new construction turned into a melodrama of the old school. For landmark-quality holdouts, a race between official designation and demolition often occurred. What was formerly a private negotiation, mostly over money between a little guy and a big guy, had become a political spectacle between the "good guys" (preservationists) and the "bad guys" (developers).

The landmark movement, which began small with New York City's 1965 law has, over the past three decades, neutralized large areas of the city from potential as development-holdout battlefields. Ironically, the destruction of the original Penn Station, an early preservation defeat, led to passage of the Landmark Preservation Law, its vindication by the United States Supreme Court in a decision that saved Grand Central Termi-

nal, and the rarity of developer victories over preservationists today.

The landmark building has a best friend no holdout can ever claim: government. The significance of this alliance was not exaggerated in a 1968 cartoon by Alan Dunn that appeared in the *New Yorker* (Figure A). The cost of relocating Grand Central Terminal as shown in the cartoon would have wound up in the holdout's pocket were there no Landmarks law.

Manhattan's building history from Peter Stuyvesant through the 1970s has largely involved the replacement of smaller buildings with larger ones. Holdouts often got in the way of this progress, since larger lots were generally required for larger structures. But with the growing fashionable example of the Landmarks law showing the way, it has become more chic to live in a converted old loft than in a new apartment. It is likely to be more affordable and better business to rent office space in a landmark such as the recycled Puck Building at Houston and Lafayette Streets, or in refitted lofts in the vicinity of the Flatiron Building at 23rd Street, than to fuel the market for new high-rise office buildings in more traditional headquarters-office locations.

The passion for recycling Manhattan

"We think Marcel Breuer really has it licked now."

buildings has severely maimed the hold-out business. The current preference for contextual building regulation means that new development should adapt its bulk and massing—some would say even its style—to its neighbors on the block. A holdout has reduced power to blackmail the new development under these rules.

Outside Manhattan, zoning regulations spurred holdout conflicts as long as open-space ratios demanded large lots for residential developments. Inevitably, these lower-density areas resented high-rises such as the 33-story Glen Oaks North Shore Towers at Grand Central Parkway in Queens and their 100-acre golf course as neighbors, no matter how large the open space that surrounds them. Unlike the central-business-district plazas, these open spaces were private and unappreciated except by the planners who had ordered them. In the later 1980s, contextual zoning replaced these regulations and permitted higher land-coverage buildings (similar to the buildings of the past), which can be built incrementally on smaller lots. Contextual zoning and designation of landmarks and historic districts reduced holdout activity in the lower-density zones.

The prevalence of holdouts reflects the scarcity of land and the intensity of competition for its use. The office building, long a consumer of prime land and one of the principal generators of holdouts, may be on its way to becoming a dinosaur. It is no longer necessary to assemble office workers in one location in order to pro-duce a product or provide services. New York's appetite for office buildings was a function of its unique mix of wealth, its port location and its supply of trained and untrained labor. Technology may have rendered large office buildings obsolete to the extent that its tasks can be put together more efficiently and at lower cost by a telecommunicative amalgamation of home workers using computers and cyberspace resources. And the residual need for occasional small office buildings is not likely to stimulate the holdout imagination with the prospect of big bucks.

Where today city government, acting through its Landmarks Preservation Commission, resolves holdout problems by putting a significant part of the city off-bounds to the developer, in the past the city attempted to sidestep holdouts by seeking increased condemnation powers. This legislative initiative was rebuffed in 1971, but seven years later, city government found new ways to become an active participant in a theatrical hold-out–developer confrontation in midtown Manhattan.

The case of 1 Park Avenue Plaza illustrates the regulatory power of government to influence the outcome of a hard negotiation between private real-estate interests. Zoning activism and timid land-marking shaped in surprising ways the denouement of a 1978 development boxing match between two dramatically different combatants.

A socially prominent and long-established upper-class New York institution, the Racquet and Tennis Club, located at 370 Park Avenue between 52nd and 53rd Streets (Figure B), emerged the victor in a development rights battle against the experienced and street-smart Larry Fisher of Fisher Brothers, who had assembled a large mid-block through lot immediately west of the Racquet Club.

Fisher wanted two things from the Racquet Club: the unused development rights over its low landmark-quality building and access through the building to gain a Park Avenue presence and address for his proposed mid-block office tower. The unused development rights were a product of the zoning rules. Under the existing zoning, the Racquet Club's lot was permitted to have on it a building whose total floor area could total 18 times the square footage of the lot. In fact, the Racquet Club's total area was only about five times the size of its lot. Zoning rules allowed the unbuilt allowable area to be transferred to the Fisher lot to the west, provided the parties could strike a deal. The Park Avenue address that Fisher craved required actual access to Park Avenue, whose frontage was occupied by the Racquet Club.

B The Racquet and Tennis Club.

The unused Racquet Club building allowance would add at least 15 floors to the Fisher tower, not an insignificant element of value; the worth of the Park Avenue address was, although less quantifiable, nonetheless clearly of significant financial benefit to Fisher's anticipated efforts to lease space in the new building. Fisher offered the club $300,000 annually for both, which after taxes did not do much for its aging building in the club's opinion. The club wanted more.

In a resourceful strategy, Fisher went instead to government to see if it would give him what the club would not. He succeeded quickly with the Manhattan Borough President, who was in charge of giving out new addresses. Even without access to Park Avenue, or an open plaza, the new building address would be known forever after as 1 Park Avenue Plaza.

The extra floors were a more difficult obstacle. Given the lot size of 45,000 square feet, the largest total floor area the city could permit on the site was 18 times the area of the lot (an 18 FAR or floor–area ratio). Since the club had thus far refused to merge its lot with Fisher's, thereby bequeathing to Fisher the unused potential floor area, the larger building was impossible via this route.

If only Fisher could persuade the City Planning Commission to crack the 18 FAR ceiling on midtown-lot development in return for building an extraordinary public amenity . . . . At the time, however, the city's first priority was to turn up a purchaser for the private Tudor City Parks' air rights 12 blocks away and establish their market value in an elaborate zoning regulation designed to preserve the parks without depriving their owner of value. Fisher offered $4 million for these air rights, but Harry Helmsley, their owner, wanted $8 million.

Rebuffed on the Tudor City possibility, Fisher came up with the concept of a block-through 60-foot-high galleria connecting 52nd and 53rd Streets, a space he likened to Milan's Galleria Vittorio Emanuele and a public space unlike any in New York City. The commission was hooked, and it amended the city's Zoning Resolution to recognize such an amenity for bonus floor-area purposes and allowed it to earn bonus buildable area up to 19.5 FAR. What's more, it granted a special permit for Fisher's 19.5 FAR tower including the galleria. Fisher had made an end run around the club and gotten the city to "print" the extra floor area without paying the club so much as a penny for its trouble or its so-called air rights.

It was now Racquet Club's turn to be creative, and it unveiled a plan to endow itself for the foreseeable future with the income from a 486-room 38-story Park Avenue hotel built on its roof! Since the club's lot extended only 100 feet to the west of the avenue, the hotel would be rather tall and thin, but with its structural supports cleverly threaded through the club's existing interior walls, the plan was feasible without even disturbing the posh and treasured indoor tennis courts that formed much of the raison d'être of the club's building. The Park Avenue views from the proposed hotel would be smashing—much better than the views enjoyed by the east-facing tenants in 44 stories of offices in 1 Park Avenue Plaza, who would face the new hotel's 38-story blank service-core rear wall (Figure C).

C Plan proposed by the Racquet Club. *(Andrew Alpern)*

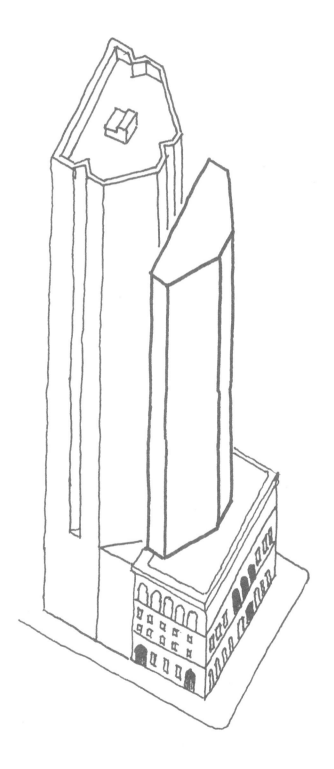

The Fishers cried uncle. They bought the Racquet Club air rights for a one-shot payment of $5 million, thus increasing the size of their zoning lot for 1 Park Avenue Plaza. This larger zoning lot greatly increased the permissible size of the building and made the extraordinary and costly 60-foot-high galleria superfluous. The galleria was accordingly sliced horizontally in half and the lower half was built as a more conventional 30-foot-high public block-through arcade. The upper half became rent-generating offices in the revised scheme.

After the shouting died down, the Racquet Club was designated a city landmark. Although designed by the eminent architectural firm of McKim, Mead & White, and clearly worthy, it had been passed over in the previous decade because of protests by the club's influential members that designation would impair the club's economic survivability. Had it been a designated landmark at the time of 1 Park Avenue Plaza—and there *was* pressure to designate—it is unlikely that the club's hotel maneuver would have seemed credible, given the aversion of the Landmarks Preservation Commission to buildings over landmarks. But without that designation, the club was able to pull off its bluff and, as an article in *New York Magazine* heralded, "A Gentlemen's Club K.O.'s The Real-Estate Kings." As the public co-respondent of the occasion, the City Planning Commission was entitled to feel both embarrassed and ill-used. Some years later, the commission quietly repealed the "Milan-galleria" provision in the Zoning Resolution.

A more effective government intervention in the holdout *v.* assemblage negotiation process occurred in 1983, just as the authors were preparing the first edition of this book for publication. It all began in an almost surreal manner as tall, ultra-thin buildings suddenly mushroomed in the nicest, highest-priced, low-rise, mid-block residential areas of Manhattan.

They were called "sliver" buildings by a hostile community: their developers were unable to assemble contiguous town-house lots and clear a large enough site on which to build a conventionally proportioned apartment house. These neighboring town houses were either landmarked, or were occupied by rent-regulated tenants who could not be evicted or by owners in residence who were loath to leave.

The city's zoning regulations were sliver-blind and allowed these holdouts to have their cake (the town house) and eat it too (*i.e.*, sell their unused development rights). A developer, in the market for an assemblage, was able to settle for one or two small footprint lots occupying less than 45 feet of mid-block frontage and

then, by acquiring the unused air rights over each neighboring town house, combine the "extra" buildable area represented by those acquired rights with the buildable area of the footprint parcel he actually owned. The result was an ungainly skinny structure towering above neighboring town houses because it had amassed development rights from a contiguous chain of neighboring underbuilt parcels (Figure D).

"Luxury," according to *Metropolis* magazine, "was a sliver building's handmaiden," since there were few economies of scale possible in a building with only one apartment per floor. Narrowness was said to add as much as 20 percent to the cost, but the New York market reservoir of wealthy and corporate purchasers and renters made such construction profitable.

In the face of vigorous condemnation of the phenomenon by vociferous public-interest groups and in the press, the City Planning Commission amended the Zoning Resolution to limit the allowable height of sliver buildings (with less than 45-foot frontage width) to the lesser of 100 feet or the width of the abutting street (usually 60 feet). Over time, the city used other zoning diet remedies to squeeze the "fat" of unused development rights out of zoning classifications in so-called contextual-development areas. This effectively took away the safety net that allowed anomalous development as a means of dealing with holdout properties.

Today, with lower-cost financing providing assistance to housing production across the country, regulatory obstacles of governments, rather than greedy holdout demands, are chiefly responsible for inhibiting residential development. New housing production in New York City has fallen to an all-time low in the 1990s. As repeatedly proclaimed by Seymour Durst, such levels of production are far below what is needed to replace and replenish the city's aged existing housing stock. In descending order of importance, significant impediments to the construction of much-needed housing are sustained by the following regulatory obstacles:

1. Inappropriate, obsolete zoning of extensive waterfront and other locations, reserving land for vanishing industrial uses and prohibiting construction of new housing.

2. The costliness of undertaking a city environmental review of this improperly zoned land, which must precede any zoning change of use according to state environmental-quality-review laws enacted 20 years ago.

3. The persistent shadow of rent-control and rent-stabilization laws, which

D 328 East 86th Street. *(Copyright 1995 Gil Amiaga)*

has inhibited new rental-housing investment.

4. The spread of historic-district and landmark designations, which has put large city areas off limits to development.

5. The complexity and extent of land use regulation on federal, state and city levels, the cost of negotiating the process and the far greater costs of changing existing regulation, notwithstanding the merit of particular changes.

Planners will criticize this list and point out the many competing values which are responsible for it. Planners advise; leaders act. Elected officials must sort out their priorities, and if new housing is one, the obstacles listed above (or at least some of them) must be removed.

In those corners of the city where market demand for land is strong and zoning permits, holdout dramas continue. For example, there has been a long-running holdout soap opera on West 57th Street. The star of this near-farce has been the Russian Tea Room. As an inducement to lure investment west of Sixth Avenue, the city created development incentives that were very attractive to the restaurant's neighbors on both sides and behind it. The owner of the restaurant played too hard to get, with the result that she found herself hemmed in by Harry Macklowe's 712-foot black-glass Metropolitan Tower to the east, Rockrose's 756-foot Carnegie Hall Tower to the west and Bruce Eichner's 810-foot CitySpire tower to the south. Thus surrounded, the unused development rights of the Russian Tea Room's 1875 building remained unproductive.

The flamboyant restaurateur Warner LeRoy bought the Russian Tea Room when longtime owner Faith Stewart Gordon retired in 1995. He then promptly closed the restaurant and auctioned off its trademark collection of samovars and year-round Christmas decorations. This left him with the still-extant development rights, which he proposed to use by demolishing the former brownstone row house, building in its place a six- or seven-story structure that could support double-height dining rooms for LeRoy's theatrical concept of what a new Russian Tea Room ought to be. He proposed an "Imperial" building façade that might have been an architect's nightmare of the Russian Revolution, and threatened to construct behind it a two-story revolving Russian bear of clear plastic with goldfish swimming inside. But even this vision of a polyester Fabergé theme park would be restrained by the 25-foot width of the existing lot. Regardless of design or embellishments, anything on the site of the venerable old restaurant holdout would still be a rather insubstantial Russian tea sandwich between its gargantuan 57th

Street neighbors (Figure E)—another architectural anomaly resulting from the actions of a holdout owner.

And so you are about to embark on an unusual tour of New York City and certain other urban landscapes transformed by holdout conflicts. The tour will include often bizarre, sometimes graceful architectural accommodations, alternatively amusing and suspenseful negotiation narratives and an illustrated primer of real-estate lore. If it strikes a "Believe It or Not" quality at times, I can only vouch for the integrity of the guides.

If the era has changed since the book's original publication, its idiosyncratic qualities stand out even more today than they did before. No sour notes of revisionism have been visited upon the text and you will have done with contemporary cant when you conclude these observations.

NORMAN MARCUS is a practicing attorney with Bachner, Tally, Polevoy & Misher who was Counsel for 20 years to the New York City Planning Commission and Department of City Planning. He is an Adjunct Professor of Land Use Law at New York University Law School and the Wagner School for Public Service. He is co-editor of *The New Zoning* (Praeger Publishers, 1970) and a contributing author to *Planning and Zoning New York City* (Center for Urban Policy Research, 1994).

E A Russian tea sandwich. *(Copyright Gil Amiaga)*

Foreword
to the First Edition
by JOHN V. LINDSAY

Cities are arenas of competing interests, as anyone who's been a mayor can attest. Thus it is no coincidence that the examination of some form of conflict lies at the heart of those books which add significantly to our understanding of how cities function. This worthwhile volume takes such a place in the literature of urban planning and design.

On one side of the conflicts described in these pages is a developer who's gained possession of a plot of land almost large enough to be the site of an office tower or apartment house he wants to build; on the other side is the owner of the remaining parcel of property the developer needs to complete his planned project's site assemblage. The property owner who, for whatever reason, does not sell that remaining parcel is known in the real estate business as a "holdout."

The outcomes of these contests of will between developers and holdouts have left an indelible imprint on New York's cityscape. The nineteenth-century townhouse on West End Avenue, flanked on either side by massive apartment buildings constructed a generation later; the restaurant that's been a midtown neighborhood landmark for decades and survives intact tucked into the ground floor of a soaring new office tower; the two-story white clapboard house that stands proudly, if conspicuously, among the concrete structures on Charles Street in Greenwich Village; the tall, down-town commercial building that is geometrically regular except for a seem-ingly inexplicable notch in its Pine Street face; and any number of sudden, sharp declivities in the skyline all memorialize the struggles between de-velopers and holdouts that have shaped the metropolis's built environ-ment.

Running like harmonies under the fascinating stories you are about to read are broad public policy choices involving the rights of private prop-erty owners and the community's need to provide for such facilities as corporate headquarters and housing units, and the passions of human nature erupting as complex transactions drive these negotiators to displays of emotion equalled only on the opera house stage.

The authors of this book generally regard holdouts as obstacles to max-imum urban economic development and housing production. While I feel that the rights of the owner of a small parcel of property are as valid as the rights of a developer who has amassed a vast adjacent plot for a major project (and as deserving of protection under the law) there is little ques-tion that contemporary municipal fiscal, social, and economic pressures all make the construction of office towers and apartment buildings of utmost importance to citydwellers.

In New York City the real estate tax base accounts for 42 percent of all locally generated revenue. Improvements in real property from construc-tion and rehabilitation activity mean higher tax assessments and, therefore, more income for the public treasury; but there are still additional streams of cash generated for the government's coffers when, say, an office tower is built. Sales taxes produced by the purchase of the building's materials, payroll taxes from construction and related employment, permanent jobs sited in the tower once it is completed, and ancillary services—such as restaurants, hotels, and retail shops—expanding their operations because of the new corporate headquarters' presence all generate livelihoods for our citizens and revenue to fund the delivery of such essential services as fire protection, a police force, and sanitation pick-ups. In the face of a contracting national economy, diminished assistance for cities from Wash-ington, and the increased costs of assuring urban residents not the amen-ities, but merely the necessities of a civilized life—relative safety from crime, a healthy environment, access to educational opportunities and decent health care, and a reliable mass transit system—the construction of a corporate headquarters and the dividends it yields give cause for cheer all around.

So does the completion of a massive apartment complex in a city whose residential vacancy rate has been mired below 3 percent, on average, for almost two decades.

To the holdout, though, the community's interests are, understandably, not the only factor to be considered.

What about the tavern or restaurant owner who can't imagine his steady clientele following the establishment to another location? P.J. Clarke's, Joe & Rose, the Reidys', and Hurley's all stand in midtown where they have been for decades because their owners elected to negotiate and remain, rather than merely take the proffered money and leave.

What about the elderly woman who has lived in the same house most of her life and fears pulling up roots at this late stage? Because of such a woman, the Macy's Department Store on Queens Boulevard wasn't built larger, nor did it have the plaza entrance its architect originally envisioned. After she died, the woman's son said, "Her house was her whole life, and we saved it for her."

No matter how compelling the larger needs of the community in these instances, one cannot be without feeling for the plight of the immigrant woman near the end of her days, or for the dilemma faced by a service business whose customers had been loyal for years.

To be sure, not all holdouts make a claim on our sympathies. There is the professional real estate holdout like Alfred King who invested in corner plots to yoke the largest possible purchase price from a developer working on an assemblage. And there is the intransigent woman whose outsized stubbornness stymied the construction of the great London Terrace complex on 23rd Street for a considerable length of time. The holdout always operates in a seller's market and many of them have tried to extract disproportionate advantage from that situation.

The motives of avarice, fear, principle, and public necessity sharply color this book's anecdotes. The conclusions of these stories are visible on the city's boulevards and sidestreets. The holdouts this book describes typically made the developer delay, scale down, or otherwise alter his original design; these changes, of course, were expensive for the developer and, in the long run, to the rest of us as well. In most of the cases given here the holdout did not frustrate the project altogether. Where a holdout prevents a building from being erected, however, there is no way of telling what the aborted development would have meant to the city.

Some holdouts maintain that by literally standing their ground, they can make as important a contribution to urban life as a new development. The smaller shop or townhouse in the appropriate location, they say, may lend a grace note of diversity to a city's architectural fabric and offer a scale certain commentators term "human."

In 1971, while I was mayor of New York City, my administration through its Department of City Planning made an effort to attain what the authors of this book yearn for; namely, ". . . some form of compromise between the individual property rights of holdout owners and the greater need of the entire city for coordinated, planned, and continued rejuvenation through a mechanism akin to zoning regulations and building laws." The Introduction of this book quotes the essence of the bill we submitted to the City Council—legislation which would have provided a means for increased real estate development and benefit for the entire city while giving just compensation to the would-be holdouts.

Our bill was rejected, but Yonkers passed one similar to it which withstood a court test. Sooner or later New York, and other cities which have yet to do so, will inevitably be forced to frame a policy addressing the conflict between developers and holdouts.

Finding ways of mediating between competing interests is one of government's most difficult and crucial responsibilities. The tensions between private rights and public purposes continue to affect the lives of every citizen. This book testifies to the force of those tensions as it illuminates the grand, if irregular, façades of a great city with its marvelous sagas and shrewd insights.

Preface

Since early in this century the Durst Organization has been active in real estate investment, primarily in the New York area. Beginning in the 1940s the thrust of this organization's activities turned to extensive site assemblages and their development with large office buildings.

The dealings attendant on these projects were usually made difficult by the emergence of holdout properties which became obstacles against these development endeavors. By the end of the 1960s the file folder documenting these problems had become sufficiently overstuffed to suggest that a book about the phenomenon might be justified.

Over the next decade, a part-time but persistent search for holdout situations produced a collection of examples that demonstrated that the effects of holdouts could be detrimental to more people than just the unfortunate builder confronted with one. When holdout stories were found which explained why certain buildings had strangely shaped floor plans and why others appeared to be incomplete, it was obvious that here was a tale which would be of interest to architects as well as real estate professionals.

But when serious and thorough research revealed the details of the holdouts' negotiations and the personalities of the holdout owners and occupants, the potential popular appeal of a book about holdouts became eminently manifest.

At first it was thought that our book would tell of holdouts throughout the United States (indeed, the Introduction includes one as far away as Israel) but detailed investigations uncovered so many in New York City alone, that we decided to restrict the scope of this volume to our favorite metropolis. We would of course welcome contributions of holdout stories from readers in other parts of the country, and will consider a companion or supplementary edition if the volume of suitable information warrants it.

The time is particularly apt for a public airing of the malevolent impact of holdouts on the face of the city, since recent changes in New York's zoning regulations are likely to shift development to the older sections of the city. With possible building sites being comprised of myriad small parcels, the potential is significant for holdouts blocking change that would be beneficial to a large segment of New Yorkers.

Thus we offer a book that we hope is entertaining and that may perhaps encourage a public awareness of holdouts that will help prevent interference with the rejuvenation of New York, which is so essential to a healthy economy. As America's First City, a financially sound New York is a keystone for a financially sound United States. If we have focused attention on an impediment to that stability then we can be satisfied that we have done our bit for our country.

Andrew Alpern
Seymour Durst

Acknowledgments

Thanks are owed to innumerable people who helped with various aspects of the development and production of this book: to Jeremy Robinson for encouraging the project and making possible its publication; to John M. Rowley for selfless research time and invaluable documentation; to Jordan Auslander for repeated forays into the records of the past; to R. Steven Hyde Miller of the Museum of the City of New York for picture research beyond what was hoped for; to Dr. James Bell and his skilled and gracious staff at the New-York Historical Society for their help and courtesies; and for assistance both general and specific, Christopher Gray, Donald Schnabel, Donald Weill, Arthur Margon, Alan Burnham, Peter Klemperer, Erin Drake Gray, Shirley Baig, Harmon Hendricks Goldstone, Pauline Baerwald Falk, James Austrian, Joseph Thanhauser, Henry Baker, Robert Kellner, Alan Goldberg, Michael Saphier, Gil Amiaga, Meredith M. Collins, Bernard Rifkin, Edward S. Gordon, Marie Corrado, Gerald Schein, Bevin Koeppel, Allen Freeman, Frederick Lightfoot, Laurie Hanson, Reid K. Taube, David Bjerklie, David Grossberg, W. Easley Hamner, Dan Aspenson, James V. Reed, R. O. Blechman, Joan Zseleczky, Phillip Shannon, Mildred Westermann, Alan Freed, Harold Kelman, and others whose lack of inclusion by name in no way diminishes the appreciation for their assistance. The quotation of Irwin Chanin is © 1930 by The New York Times Company and is reprinted by permission.

Introduction

Construction activity in New York is so commonplace that it is taken virtually for granted. Old buildings come down, giant excavations are blasted and dug, foundations are poured, and new structures grow at a prodigious production pace. Sidewalk superintendents watch the progress; newspapers chronicle the construction milestones and occasionally the disastrous mishaps; and old-time New Yorkers sometimes sigh with nostalgia over some favorite landmark that has disappeared. When the construction crews have left, the critics take over and the new buildings are admired or cursed . . . or ignored.

But it is the new construction that gets the attention. Seldom noticed, and often quite invisible, are the impediments to that construction. There are many obstacles that can impede the progress of a real estate development, but perhaps none can be as time-consuming, expensive, or frustrating as a holdout.

A holdout does not happen in the natural course of events, and it does not occur by chance. It is the result of a deliberate course of action taken by a landowner, or by one who holds a lease on a piece of property. A holdout property owner who demands an excessive price can force a developer to increase rents in the new building to cover increased costs. A completely unrealistic demand can totally doom a project, or it can force a contorted architectural solution in order to avoid the holdout. It can delay planning or construction work, that in itself increasing project carrying costs, and can kill a development if protracted. Holdouts are the bane of any developer's existence, but they also work to the detriment of the new building's occupants when they result in higher rents, and to the public when they do visual damage to the streetscape.

Holdout Types

People who are holdouts come in several varieties. Most pathetic is the frightened holdout. The woman who has lived in the same place for fifty years and is panicked by the idea of being uprooted; the father who is worried that no landlord will accept his retarded son; the successful restauranteur who is afraid of failure at a new location. With tact, imagination, and persistence, however, the frightened holdout can be won over.

Then there is the greedy holdout, who thinks that every developer controls a purse of unlimited depth and that no price is too high to demand. This rapaciousness is likely to kill a project, or it may leave this owner's property high and dry while development goes on all around.

There is a very small group of real estate people who are professional holdouts. One of the first was Alfred King, who bought small corner buildings on blocks he felt were ripe for development. He didn't try to hide his purchases, since he would set his "holdout price," usually double the going market value, and sit back to wait for a developer willing to assemble a larger site which needed his corner property. While his price would be high, he didn't haggle. His price was firm, and if you were willing to pay it, you got the deed. He was known as "King for Corners," and he would occasionally paint his name on the side of his buildings by way of advertising (Figure 3).

Finally, there is the foolish holdout. Motivated by spite, by a need to defy anyone in a position of perceived power or authority, by a desire for publicity or notoriety, or by sheer cussedness, this sort of holdout is perhaps the most difficult to deal with because he cannot be reached with reason, and will not respond to rational offers. Some of the most visible holdout structures that blight the orderly architectural development of the urban center of the city are caused by owners of this type who cannot see the futility of their positions and the self-destructive nature of their demands.

Doris Gagnon: A Holdout on a Beach

Colorful holdouts don't necessarily have to occupy buildings slated for demolition in order to attract attention, although some connection to a structure appears to be essential. Persistence, together with a penchant for zaniness, would seem to be all that is needed for a successful holdout.

Doris Gagnon is just such a holdout. In 1951, she moved into a cottage on the Silver Sands Beach at Milford, Connecticut. In 1959, the Silver Sands Beach State Park was proposed, and eviction of all residents of the site began. Ten years later, all had left except Mrs. Gagnon. Then in 1971, after all other efforts had failed, the state's Department of Environmental Protection bulldozed Mrs. Gagnon's home while she was away at work. The woman's response to this turn of events landed her in jail for two months, after which she was confined to a mental hospital.

Upon her release, Mrs. Gagnon returned to her property and lived in her car. When state authorities attempted to bar her by blocking her roadway, she tore out the impediments, gaining her fifteen more days of incarceration. She kept returning nonetheless, "like some damned pesky weed," according to a local governmental minion, and gradually

1 A holdout that has become a survivor. This building at the corner of 50th Street and Ninth Avenue was a holdout at the time the entire block was being assembled for development. By the time the building was acquired and vacated, the development plans had been shelved and the land put to temporary use as a parking lot. Since the increased income from a few additional parking spaces is not sufficient to justify the costs of demolition, this decrepit structure will remain until construction of a new project to improve the block is begun. *(Andrew Alpern)*

2 When viewed from a more southerly vantage point, the derelict holdout at 50th Street and Ninth Avenue seems forlorn among a sea of parked cars. *(Courtesy of The Durst Organization)*

3 Professional holdout Alfred King often liked to advertise his holdings. This sign at 49th Street and Ninth Avenue appears on the north face of a tenement building he once owned. *(Andrew Alpern)*

erected a residential complex comprising three cars, three house trailers, a dog house, a tent, and a chicken coop.

A local police officer was quoted as telling state officials, "You're never going to get rid of her; you're going to wind up calling this place the Doris Gagnon State Park." The state park was never constructed and there are no present plans to build one. Mrs. Gagnon is still there, however, with little likelihood that anyone will ever be able to dislocate her.

A Five-Inch Holdout

The most truly invisible holdouts are those whose insistence on obtaining unrealistic prices for their property completely dooms assemblages and development projects. A particularly absurd case involved a strategically placed piece of land only 5 inches wide.

Narrow strips of land are generally the result of inaccurate surveys or imprecise deed descriptions. Ordinarily these are brought to light during the searches conducted by title insurance companies, and property-line agreements are drawn up between owners of adjacent lots to resolve the discrepan-

cies. Occasionally, the city lays claim to these "ownerless" strips and auctions them off to real estate speculators. Every so often an amateur gets into the act.

Such was the case on March 23, 1953, when taxi driver Christopher Giaimo attended a city auction and bought a strip of land 5 inches wide and 78 feet deep separating 1086 Second Avenue from 1088, between 57th and 58th Streets. Mr. Giaimo liked the fact that his new property was right around the corner from the four-story 22-foot-wide apartment house he owned and lived in at 306 East 58th Street. And he particularly liked the price: $225.

Veteran real estate investor Henry Baker already owned 1086 Second Avenue as well as two adjoining buildings on 57th Street. Hoping to create an assemblage of sufficient size for economic development, Mr. Baker approached the taxi driver, laid his cards on the table, and asked what the price would be for the 5-inch strip. Mr. Giaimo demanded $40,000, or $1230 per square foot—a record for the time. Rather than lower his price when Mr. Baker attempted to negotiate, the amateur investor asserted that he would just as soon erect a lamp

post on his land with his name on it, conveniently ignoring the fact that his strip of land was already inaccessible under the encroachments of the adjoining buildings. Mr. Baker considered that meeting Mr. Giaimo's price would not be practical, so he dropped his development plans, later selling what he had already acquired to an investment group headed by Edwin Glickman.

The Glickman group was more interested in removing Mr. Giaimo from the block, since it had already developed plans for a huge apartment house on the block-long site. Following a marathon negotiating session with the taxi driver in 1956, the Glickman interests arranged a tax-free exchange, worth $75,000, by which Mr. Giaimo traded his four-story house and the 5-inch strip for a five-story house nearby at 331 East 58th Street. The group then erected The Excelsior—a grandiose apartment tower atop a base of commercial and retail space. The building was subsequently converted to cooperative ownership, yielding a significant profit to the original builders. Christopher Giaimo still lives on 58th Street and is pleased with the deal he struck. Henry Baker is in his

An architectural rendering of the Astor House prepared before the construction work had begun. The Barclay Street corner of the building, at the right, was the site of the holdout house of John G. Costar. (*Collection of Andrew Alpern*)

nineties and is still active in real estate dealings, but he regrets that his development plans for the site were thwarted by the demands of a neophyte land speculator seeking a huge profit.

John Jacob Astor Encounters a Holdout In 1834

An early holdout temporarily crimped the development plans of the first John Jacob Astor, variously described as New York's Landlord, and The City's Richest Citizen. Having reached the biblical age of three score and ten in the early 1830s, Mr. Astor sought a means of memorializing himself. His home was at Broadway and Vesey Street, which he considered a fashionable place to be. Reasoning that others might also want to dwell there, at least temporarily, he determined to erect a grand hotel at that location. He quietly bought the lots he needed to complete the blockfront, but encountered an obstacle when he attempted to buy the house of John G. Costar at 227 Broadway on the corner of Barclay Street. Mr. Astor offered the fair market value of $30,000 for the house but Mr. Costar, also getting on in years, refused the bid. An offer of $40,000 was similarly rejected. Mr. Costar had called the house his home for many years, and since he had no need for additional cash, he saw no reason to leave.

Seeing that he had no alternative, Mr. Astor revealed to Mr. Costar his plans for a hotel. He explained that Mr. Costar's lot was all that was needed for him to be able to begin construction, and he asked Mr. Costar to name his own price. The figure $60,000 was given, conditioned on the consent of Mrs. Costar, which could be sought the following morning. When Mr. Astor came calling, he was received cordially and was graciously told by the old lady, "I don't want to sell the house, but we are such old friends that I am willing for your sake." Mr. Astor was said to have later related the story with wry humor, asserting that anyone could afford to exhibit such condescension when one is assured of receiving double the value of a piece of property.

Designed by architect Isaiah Rogers and planned originally with the name of the Park Hotel, the building took two years to construct and was opened in 1836 (Figure 4). Even before it was completed, the hotel was known as Astor House in the newspapers of the day, and the name stuck. For many years, Astor House enjoyed popularity as a particularly fashionable hostelry, but the uptown growth of the city gradually left it behind. The southern half was demolished in 1915 for an office building, and the northern portion met a similar fate not long after.

The Little House: A Holdout Story for Children

The concept of a holdout has been considered a suitable topic for a children's book. In 1942, Virginia Lee Burton wrote and illustrated a charming little volume titled *The Little House*. Its protagonist is a pretty little house that was built around the middle of the nineteenth century "way out in the country" by a man who constructs it sufficiently soundly to last for his "great-great-grandchildren's great-great-grandchildren." He vows that it will "never be sold for gold or silver," thus creating a hereditary holdout.

As the years go by, the city gradually encroaches upon the neighboring countryside until the little house finds itself surrounded first with tenement houses, and then trolly cars, and an elevated train, and a subway, and finally overwhelmed on both sides by tall office buildings. Unable to be sold, the house languishes and falls prey to vandals and neglect (Figure 5).

Since it is a children's book, there is ultimately a happy ending for the poor little house. The great-great-granddaughter of the man who built it decides that it needs a new lease on life, but since she can't sell it "for gold or silver," she jacks up the house, puts it onto a flatbed trailer truck, and carts it back out to the country. She and the little house presumably live happily ever after . . . and the holdout site in the middle of the city is released for more appropriate development (Figure 6).

Life imitated art when the old clapboard "little house" in a backyard at 71st Street and York Avenue was trucked down to a countrylike vacant lot on Charles Street in Greenwich Village, allowing the uptown site to be appropriately redeveloped (see Figure 108, pp. 80–81). Such happy compromises don't happen often.

Skyscraper: A Broadway Show about a Holdout

The quintessential New York holdout was made the subject of a musical comedy which opened at the Lunt-Fontanne Theatre on Broadway in the fall of 1965. Based on *Dream Girl*, by Elmer Rice, *Skyscraper* is the story of the young owner of a brownstone with an antiques shop on the ground floor, and the builder who wants to buy her property to complete the site for his new office building.

Georgina Allerton lives alone in a building she perceives to be of great historical importance. She is a leader in the fight to preserve historical buildings in New York and she dreams of being awarded the Pulitzer Prize in urban prevention. Bushman Construction Company has already begun construction of a mammoth skyscraper next door, and wants to buy her brownstone. Older brother Bert Bushman cannot understand why she won't accept his offer of $150,000 for the deed, although his younger brother Tim has second thoughts about the project. An architect by profession, Tim is afraid that the "pimply" metal exterior of the new building will give the city of New York a case of acne. Tim encounters Georgina, who mistakes him for a construction worker and demands to know why the construction company has cut off her electricity and punctured her gas pipes.

5 The fictional Little House suffering as an enforced holdout by the encroachments of the developing city. *(Virginia Lee Burton, courtesy of Houghton Mifflin Company)*

6 In a last-minute rescue to save the house from total destruction, its owner moves the diminutive structure out to the countryside, preserving the holdout building while relinquishing its site. *(Virginia Lee Burton, courtesy of Houghton Mifflin Company)*

5

6

Although Tim denies any wrongdoing, he is attracted to Georgina and asks her out to dinner. Georgina of course considers him to be the enemy and refuses the invitation.

Georgina goes back to her antiques shop, where she and her part-time assistant Roger are visited by Bert Bushman, who raises his offer for the brownstone to $165,000, an offer Georgina angrily refuses. Tim Bushman follows his brother into the shop and again tries to make a date with Georgina, who by now is having doubts about her resolve to keep the unproductive antiques shop. After courting her by hanging from a construction crane outside her window, Tim finally succeeds in obtaining Georgina's consent to have dinner with him.

Following dinner, Tim takes her atop the steel girders of the new building and tells her about its development, and the growth of the city all around her. He shows her how important progress is to the city and its people and, since this is Broadway, he asks her to marry him. Deciding to stop living in a dream world and to try to turn her dreams into reality, Georgina marries Tim. They spend their wedding night in her old brownstone, and the following day abandon it to the wreckers.

Skyscraper starred Julie Harris and had a modest success (Figure 7). Its basic theme of developers and holdouts, however, has had a much larger cast and has had a much more mixed performance record.

Holdouts as Humor

The holdout as a subject for humor extends farther than the Broadway stage. It can be worked into a commercial advertisement, with the caption added later (Figure 8), or into a captionless cartoon (Figure 9). And it has inspired poets and worse.

7 The original advertising poster for *Skyscraper* showing the little brownstone at the lower left completely surrounded by the steelwork for the new office tower. *(Courtesy of Feuer and Martin and Capital Records EMI)*

8 Don't sell yet, you said.
Hold out, you said.
Demand a higher price, you said.
They can't build without our property, you said.
Well?

(USF&G Insurance)

9 A developer's ultimate patience. *(Charles Addams, courtesy of* The New Yorker*)*

The Holdout

My brick heap—how I cursed it!
(I curse myself today.)
For 15 years I nursed it
And never made it pay.

I wanted to get rid of
The blunder I had made,
But none would make a bid of
The paltry price I'd paid.

Each moment since I bought it,
I suffered in self-blame,
Yet, note—when someone sought it,
A genius I became.

"Assemblage!" I heard whispered.
My jaw went slack at this;
Incredible how this word
Can pique one's avarice.

No price they offered pleased me,
I sent them on their way,
The happy thought had seized me
That any price they'd pay.

I pictured my retirement
To some Tahitian beach
And thus my prices higher went
Each time they tried to reach.

Then one day they stopped calling,
One needn't wonder why,
The silence was appalling
And mortified was I.

I'm locked in rather badly
And going slowly mad.
I'd sell today—and gladly—
At half the price I had.

Behold the hopeless holdout
Hark well, but do not grieve;
Lord knows I should have sold out,
When fortune touched my sleeve!

I should have been more willing
To sell my property.
I could have made a killing—
Instead it's killing me!

by Don Weill

An Arab Holdout in Israel

Because of its continual level of intense development, New York City has provided an appropriate battleground for a wide variety of holdout situations, and many of these have been chronicled in this book. But of course holdouts can emerge anywhere in the world, and they are not restricted to providing harassment only to professional real estate developers. In 1980, Prime Minister Menachem Begin of Israel made plans to move his offices to a large building in East Jerusalem but was thwarted by a holdout. Only 6 feet away from the building was the land and home of Mrs. Zeinab Abu Taha, a 55-year-old Palestinian. Sharing her small stone farmhouse with fourteen other Arabs, Mrs. Abu Taha had occupied the spot for more than thirty years and vowed she would never move.

A Woman on Long Island

Jan Bradt of Smithtown, Long Island, was similarly successful in resisting the taking of her home for a pittance to provide a site for a town ballfield (which of course was never built). She battled for fourteen years and was finally awarded $2 million for the property that Smithtown officials had attempted to take for only $20,000.

A Church Strikes a Compromise in Denver

In Denver, Colorado, a battle between a developer and a local church resulted in a compromise in which both sides appear to have won. The Holy Ghost Catholic Church erected a simple sanctuary in Denver in 1924 and expanded it in 1943. Together with a small rectory, the church occupied 25,000 square feet of a 47,000 square foot triangular block at 19th and California Streets. It established a firm foothold among Denver's Catholics and felt securely ensconced in its eclectic, renaissance-style edifice, although its rectory was proving too snug for the church's expanding activities.

The Dikeou family, longtime Denver residents and developers, assembled the nonchurch portion of the triangular site for improvement, but realized that it would have to control the entire block if effective use was to be made of its property. Initial meetings with church officials quickly established that Holy Ghost had no intention of moving from the site or vacating its church building. Faced with such an intractable holdout, the Dikeous joined forces with the Lawder Corporation, a consortium of British firms, and negotiated a compromise beneficial to both God and mammon.

The final agreement gave the developers the deed to the church's property, enabling the zoning space allowance for the entire block to be used almost totally for the office structure, thus yielding a taller and more lucrative tower (Figure 10). The developer was also able to provide a suitable plaza for the new building by razing the old rectory (Figure 11). The price of the land transfer was $11 million. Besides that sum, the church obtained a 1000-year lease on its building at an annual rental of $1, and the promise of new and expanded rectory space at some nearby location.

Although this arrangement has pleased the church fathers, and presumably has satisfied the development joint venture, the resultant office building has a peculiarly shaped floor plan of minimal size. The north face of the building has a huge concave cutout which has been faceted to provide the potential for many windowed offices on each floor, but this holdout-wraparound-shape precludes the possibility of any large spaces on any of the floors of the tower, thus severely restricting its effectiveness for many potential tenants (Figure 12).

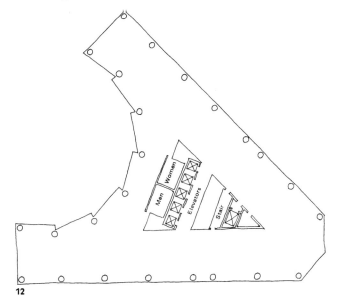

10 The entrance-front of the 1999 Broadway office tower in Denver, Colorado. There is nothing on this side of the structure to indicate that it is anything other than a conventional commercial buidling. *(Carl J. Dalio, renderer; C. W. Fentress and Associates, architect)*

11 The rear of 1999 Broadway showing how the office building wraps around the holdout church structure. *(Carl J. Dalio, renderer; C. W. Fentress and Associates, architect)*

12 A plan of the typical floor of 1999 Broadway.

Two Problems for a Gambling Casino in Atlantic City

In Atlantic City, New Jersey, two unconnected holdouts added yet another thorn to the side of Bob Guccione, publisher of *Penthouse* magazine, and would-be developer of the Penthouse Casino, a project aborted in midstream.

From the turn of the century until the beginning of the World War II, Atlantic City was a lavish, boisterous, and busy center of vacationers who sought the pleasures of the splendid beach and the elaborate and varied entertainments thoughtfully (and lucratively) provided by a virtual army of large- and small-time entrepreneurs. On the ocean at the southern end of New Jersey, Atlantic City was known as the "playground of the world" and lived up to its name by providing luxurious hotels, elaborate performances, an opulant boardwalk, and "sporting houses" said to be the best this side of Paris.

After the war, the crowds didn't come back. The mood of the country seemed to have changed, and what had formerly been enticing now looked tawdry. Atlantic City went steadily downhill, the once-grand hotels deteriorating, the vendors boarding up their booths, and the economic base of the city disappearing. After thirty years of decline, and mostly out of desperation, a referendum was passed in November 1976 to legalize casino gambling. Spearheaded by Resorts International, whose casino in the Bahamas is immensely profitable, a frantic race began, to create what was perceived to be a suitable environment in which the anticipated hoards of gamblers might drop the dollars that would presumably revitalize Atlantic City.

In 1978 Penthouse International bought the Holiday Inn and the Four Seasons Motel and announced plans to extend and connect the two hostelries and create a huge casino/hotel. The agents of this lavish sex-and-opulance empire methodically bought the quaint old buildings that separated the two old resort structures. Paying $100,000 to $150,000 for modest homes assessed at $15,000 to $20,000, they had little difficulty in obtaining the deeds they sought . . . until confronted by Vera Coking and Antoinetta Bongiovanni. Mrs. Coking was the owner of a small twenty-two-room hotel called the Sea Shell Guest House, while Mrs. Bongiovanni occupied an even more modest two-story dwelling.

Mrs. Bongiovanni flatly refused to sell to the casino interests. She had lived in her diminutive home for twenty-five years, and according to her nephew,

13

Mario Formica, "She just didn't want to move; that's all" (Figure 13).

Mrs. Coking was more of a challenge, since she negotiated with the Penthouse people for several months. She later asserted that she had never been offered more than $90,000 for her little guest house, but contemporary accounts reported that she had spurned a proffered $400,000, insisting that she wanted $4 million. When the promise of an ocean-view suite in the new hotel and free meals for the rest of her life in addition to the selling price failed to budge the stubborn woman, the developers gave up (Figure 14).

Foundations were then poured and a structural steel framework erected around the houses of both Mrs. Coking and Mrs. Bongiovanni. The disruptions caused by the construction work were evidently more than Mrs. Bongiovanni's husband could endure; he died a few months later. Mrs. Coking fared little better, her paying guests being driven away by the incessant noise of the builder's machinery and activity. The city then rubbed salt into her wounds by increasing her tax assessment from $21,000 to $111,000, an action which she fought in the courts without success.

In an ironic twist of fate, the Penthouse enterprise was not completed because of the inability of its management to make appropriate financing arrangements. Mrs. Coking and Mrs. Bongio-

14

13 The diminutive home of Antoinetta Bongio-vanni in Atlantic City surrounded by the steel-work of the Penthouse International casino, whose developers were unable to buy the little house. *(Gregory Heisler, courtesy of* LIFE *Magazine Picture Service)*

14 Vera Coking's Sea Shell Guest House overshadowed by the surrounding construction activity: a self-defeating stubbornness. *(Allen Freeman)*

vanni certainly cannot be blamed for the failure of the project, but their actions may have exacerbated the stress under which the developers were working. In the last analysis, nobody gained from the holdout situation. Mrs. Bongiovanni has become a virtual recluse, and Mrs. Coking is a bitter old woman. They gained a momentary notoriety, but their victories over the builders were hollow. One national magazine described the home of Mrs. Bogiovanni in 1979 as "a shrine to the domestic virtues—a brave little candle in a big naughty world." Pious sounding prose, perhaps, but not reflective of the realities of living with the consequences of being an intractable holdout against the more-than-reason-

able offers of legitimate real estate developers.

Antiholdout Legislation

Holdouts have created problems for builders, almost since the beginning of urban development. Delaying construction (or stopping it completely), and increasing costs, the holdout owner has been alternately glorified as the last bastion of individual free enterprise against powerful cartels, and vilified as the selfish, reactionary, antisocial exploiter of real estate. Each holdout situation is individual, of course, and the truth lies at one time or another at all points along the line connecting these two extremes.

Holdouts are really neither good nor bad; in the final analysis they are merely a phenomenon which must be dealt with.

A 1930 Proposal

Legislative solutions to the problem have been proposed on a number of occasions. In 1930, developer Irwin S. Chanin pointed out that the rejuvenation of New York was becoming increasingly difficult. The current practice of large-scale projects, he said, was often thwarted by a single obstinate owner, to the detriment of both the builder and the entire city. Mr. Chanin proposed that some legal process be initiated that would enable a developer to complete an assemblage while of course protecting the financial interests of any holdouts.

Said Mr. Chanin:

Modern building practice has demonstrated the economy of large-scale operation, but it is a tremendously difficult task to assemble an entire block of property anywhere on the Island of Manhattan. It is seldom, except when some old and large holding comes into the market, that an operation involving an entire block of property is at all possible. This is due mainly to the fact that the last property owner always holds out for the ultimate dollar, for which he cannot be blamed under the present system—or flatly refuses to be drawn into negotiations of any kind. A lesser factor is the fact that much New York real estate is constantly in litigation or so involved that no title can be given.

One person frequently makes impossible an operation which would be a vast improvement economically and which would provide employment to several thousand persons for a period of a year or more and then would add several millions of dollars to the city's assessed valuation. I am fully aware that any procedure which would involve the condemnation of property for private improvement is a blow to our long-established conception of the sacredness of private property, and yet we already have invaded that privacy with restrictions upon the use of property through the Building Code and the zoning laws, both of which are considered necessary to the public good.

It is one of the ironies of New York real estate history that owners who have blocked large developments seldom have disposed of their property for the price formerly offered by those seeking to assemble a plot. The general result of the present condition is that any effort to assemble a building plot must now be carried on with the utmost secrecy, through many and diverse brokers, generally unknown to each other.

With distressing frequency the effort to assemble a plot collapses after a year or more of heartbreaking effort, and in the rare instances where it is successfully assembled a disproportionately large amount has usually gone into the purchase of the last parcel. This may be called one of the speculations of real estate. It also enhances the costs of building which must be passed on in the form of rents to the ultimate consumer.

It is my opinion that the real estate interests of New York must make a thorough study of this situation. From the legal standpoint it probably will require a constitutional amendment backed up by appropriate legislation which will safeguard the owner, probably by permitting condemnation proceedings only to secure a small percentage of the total plot after the balance of the desired land has been obtained in the regular manner, and due effort to complete the plot by friendly purchase has failed.

Building in New York in the next few years must shift to the large areas of antiquated three to five story residential structures now situated on the middle west side from Ninth Avenue west to the Hudson River, and along a large share of the east side between Third Avenue and the East River. The average block in these districts consists of thirty to forty pieces of property held by as many persons. The value to the city at large of some legal aid in the assembling of these thousands of small holdings for large-scale modern rehabilitation is readily apparent.

A 1971 Proposal

Such legislation was introduced in New York City in 1971 in the form of an amendment to the administrative code of the city. The amendment, which was defeated, would have created a central business development district in which the city would be empowered to acquire by condemnation small parcels of property within otherwise assembled land tracts to enable development to proceed in accordance with a development plan previously approved by both the City Planning Commission and the Board of Estimate.

The support document filed with the legislation gave this background, explanation, and justification.

Major private development in New York City's central business district frequently flounders from inability to acquire a small but key parcel of land. These "holdouts" often consist of structures containing uses which are non-conforming under the city's zoning resolution or which are otherwise incompatible with the goals of the city's comprehensive plan or with a development plan for the particular area. The holdout's persistent refusal to sell its interest, even at a figure that exceeds fair market value, often obstructs such development.

This bill would permit New York City to acquire by condemnation, if necessary, incompatible or non-conforming holdouts where a substantial private assemblage of land has occurred within a defined area in the Borough of Manhattan, south of 59th Street and where the City, through its Planning Commission and the Board of Estimate, has approved after public hearing a development plan for the area comprising the private assemblage and the holdout interest. One required finding of the redevelopment plan concerns inclusion therein of specified substantial public amenities.

After approval of the plan and acquisition of the affected holdout interests, the City would be authorized to convey such interests for full consideration to the owner of the assembled area subject to the controls imposed by the City through the development plan.

Apart from the elimination of substandard and incompatible land use conditions, this bill promises the development of prime areas within the Manhattan central business district in conformity with the zoning resolution, the city's comprehensive plan, and the district's development plans. This measure can be expected to expedite private development in the public interest at no cost to the City and would have the added benefit of increasing municipal tax revenues and the economic vitality of the district, the city, and the state.

Accordingly, the Mayor urges upon the Legislature the earliest possible favorable consideration of this proposal.

An Antiholdout Law in Yonkers

Such a law was successfully enacted for the city of Yonkers which lies directly to the north of New York. The Yonkers Community Development Agency was chartered by the state legislature under the General Municipal Law, and is empowered to condemn private property for use by private or public developers when such a taking of land can be justified by establishing "a greater public purpose."

In 1975, the Community Development Agency became embroiled in a dispute with a group of local landowners. The Agency, seeking land for a proposed expansion of one of Yonkers's largest employers, the Otis Elevator Company, condemned several small commercial properties in a "blighted area" near the site of the existing Otis factory. Under a complicated federal urban renewal law, the Development Agency was reimbursed part of its cost of acquiring the land for Otis. The owners of the condemned property charged that this urban renewal legislation allowed the taking of only "substandard" property, which theirs was not, and that further, the purpose for which the land would be used would be the private profit of Otis Elevator, and not "a greater public purpose."

The case eventually reached the Court of Appeals, the highest level of state court. That tribunal affirmed the decision of the Appellate Division, Second Department, and faulted the landowners on both points. The Court held that the owners had failed to prove that their property was not substandard. The Court also held that a public purpose can be served by urban renewal clearing that aids a private company. "There is nothing malevolent about that," the Court said, referring to the Development Agency's clearance for a private company. In addition, the Court said that "Otis's on-going economic importance to the community" serves a sufficiently public need that outweighs any minor irregularities that attended the condemnation of property in the blighted area.

This decision established the principle that the profit motives of a private company are not necessarily incompatible with the public function of a redevelopment agency charged with slum clearance.

The city of Yonkers spent many millions of dollars in obtaining the land Otis wanted for its expansion, but not long after, Otis was acquired by the United Technologies Company—a corporation based in Connecticut—which decided to close the Yonkers plant, expansion and all. Yonkers responded with a lawsuit to prevent the closing, thereby attempting to maintain the local employment base and protect its investment in the area's redevelopment. The case has not yet fully been resolved.

A Similar Law in Kansas City

The state of Missouri and the city of Kansas City have enacted laws similar to the one affirmed in Yonkers, New York. In Kansas City, redevelopment by private interests acting primarily in the quest of profits can be assisted through selective public taking of holdout property. This can be accomplished through the power of eminent domain, and provision is made for payment to the owners of the land being taken. A crucial prerequisite for a forced sale of a holdout is that it be in some way "blighted" according to the definitions of the law. The law defines what constitutes a blighted area, and says that any property within such an area is subject to being taken by the city. Even if an individual piece of property is not itself blighted, it can be treated as if it were so long as it is located within an otherwise blighted area. The Kansas City law defines a blighted area as being

those portions of the city which the council shall determine, that by reason of age, obsolescence, inadequate or outmoded design or physical deterioration, have become economic and social liabilities and that the conditions in such localities are conducive to ill health, transmission of disease, crime, or inability to pay reasonable taxes.

Subsequent to enactment of the Missouri and Kansas City laws, further efforts were mounted to obtain legislation that would aid private developers in New York to deal effectively with holdout properties, but thus far nothing of any substance has emerged.

The Persistent Problem of Holdouts

Perhaps holdouts will always be with us. Since holdouts are people—albeit difficult ones—each generation is likely to create new ones. But ultimately, a fair and balanced way of dealing with these problems must be developed if the city is not to suffer through the destruction of important parts of its architectural heritage when large-scale "landmarks" provide the only practical building sites. With small holdouts making site assemblages more and more difficult, developers will stop bothering to attempt projects in the more blighted areas of the city, since these are precisely the blocks whose ownership is fragmented among amateur investors and property holders.

The Loss of Two Grand Old Hotels

Nathan Silver pointed out this problem in his book, *Lost New York*. Speaking of the old Hotel Astor on Times Square, he says,

The loss of a splendid hotel like the Astor (now the site of the office building at 1515 Broadway) is a matter for public concern in New York. The site was acquired in a single property deal, rather than expensively assembled bit by bit, and this explains why one of the most valuable buildings for blocks around was torn down, instead of some of the shabby buildings nearby.

He goes on to say that

The old Waldorf-Astoria met its end in a typical New York way: since the entire block was already under one ownership, it was cheaper for the builders of the future Empire State Building to buy it than to try to acquire nearby

property piecemeal. One of the city's most valuable buildings consequently was demolished in 1929.

Professional Planners Speak Out Against Holdouts

This problem was echoed by the Regional Plan Association in its 1969 book, *Urban Design Manhattan*. According to the association:

Large-scale land assemblage is impracticable without power of condemnation. With some few exceptions on the edges of central business districts, there are no single-fee holdings in them of more than a single block in area. Even single-block ownership is a rarity. The opportunity for private enterprise to assemble a site suitable for another Grand Central or Rockefeller Center does not exist. The bargaining power of holdouts has collapsed many projects at even the single-building scale.

Perhaps the concept of urban renewal, where condemnation powers are justified by the public interest in improving blighted areas, will be extended by redefinition of what constitutes "blight."

Decision-making is secretive. Because of the competitive nature of the real estate business generally and the holdout problem in particular, private developments in central business districts are carried on under a cloak of secrecy. Secrecy can be devastating to planning and cooperation between developers, both private and public.

A Final Word

Until it is recognized that the sustained vitality of the city requires some form of compromise between the individual property rights of holdout owners and the greater need of the entire city for coordinated, planned, and continual rejuvenation through a mechanism akin to zoning regulations and building laws, we can only call attention to some of the holdout situations that have arisen here in New York and hope that by this exposure, the problems of holdouts will reach a greater audience.

R.H. Macy & Company at Herald Square

Late in the nineteenth century the shopping hub of New York City was continuing its relentless march northward and was fast leaving 14th Street and proceeding up Sixth Avenue toward 23rd Street. Already Benjamin Altman, Hugh O'Neil, and the Ehrich Brothers had their stores between 18th and 23rd Streets, and before the old century turned into the new, Simpson-Crawford, Adams Drygoods, and Siegel-Cooper had joined them. The Siegel-Cooper store was particularly magnificent, with a pair of two-story-high bronze columns at the grandiose entrance on Sixth Avenue and a 70-foot-wide marble fountain in the center of the store surrounding an 18-foot marble statue by Daniel Chester French. The building was one of the largest in New York at the time it opened in 1896 and represented a significant investment on the part of the store's president, Henry Siegel.

Observing the movements of their competitors, Jesse and Percy Straus, owners of R. H. Macy & Company, decided that the 14th Street area their store had served since 1858 should be abandoned for more lucrative pastures further north. Correctly foreseeing a future shift of the retail center even beyond 23rd Street, they set their sights on 34th Street, where Sixth Avenue crosses Broadway. In an attempt to acquire the land they needed at reasonable cost, they began to buy the block between 34th and 35th Streets and between Broadway and Seventh Avenue, purchasing one parcel at a time through brokers acting as fronts and through straw purchasers whose purpose was to hide the identity of the true buyers—the Straus family. Included in the assemblage was the famous entertainment house of Koster and Bial, where the first crude motion pictures were shown to an amazed public in 1896. While putting together the land for the store itself, Macy's also bought two lots on the north side of 35th Street occupied at the time by the Pekin and the Tivoli, two of the more notorious bawdy houses in a city then famous for its lavish brothels. The original intent had been to build the boiler rooms for the store on the separate 35th Street plot, but this plan was later scrapped in favor of integrating the mechanical equipment within the store building itself.

Despite their efforts to maintain secrecy, the Straus and Macy names became known in connection with the real estate negotiations, bringing their acquisition plans open to public scrutiny. When the cat was out of the bag, they still hadn't bought the corner building. This tiny parcel, a mere 30 feet by 50 feet, was owned by the Reverend Alfred Duane Pell, of an old-time New York family, whose father had bought it thirty years earlier for $30,000. Dr. Pell was on a visit in Europe at the time Macy's was attempting to buy his property, but via letters and cablegrams, he agreed to sell it for $250,000 (Figure 15).

At this point, Henry Siegel, owner of the Siegel-Cooper Dry Goods Store, entered the picture. Having recently spent a great deal of money on his own new store at 18th Street, he feared that the new Macy's store would siphon the old 14th Street customers away and jeopardize his business. He hit upon the idea of taking over the old Macy's building after the Straus brothers moved their operation to 34th Street. He would immediately open a Siegel-Cooper store there, hoping in the process to acquire the old Macy's customers as well. Realizing that Macy's would resist this move, he felt that the Pell property could serve as a vehicle of persuasion.

Siegel turned to the owner of R. Smith and Company. Pop Smith was a clever merchant and a neighbor of the 14th Street Macy's store. Whenever Macy's would run an advertisement in the newspapers, Mr. Smith would stock his show windows with the same items, and customers bound for Macy's would see his displays and buy from him instead. It tickled his fancy to take on Macy's, and he agreed to serve as Siegel's undercover agent.

Henry Siegel Creates a Holdout The Reverend Pell was on his way home to trade his property to Macy's for $250,000, but Mr. Smith discovered which boat he was sailing on, and met him at the pier. Within the hour Dr. Pell had sold instead to Mr. Smith, for $375,000. Mr. Smith in turn sold to Mr. Siegel, who then attempted to negotiate with the Strauses. Much to his dismay, they refused to buy the corner building and moreover elected to keep their 14th Street building vacant for the two years remaining on their lease, rather than risk losing customers by turning it over to Mr. Siegel. They held on to the lease to the very end, not even permitting the Siegel contractors to enter the premises to make their surveys until the day the leasehold expired in 1903.

Meanwhile, Macy's was faced with the problem of the missing corner for its building plot (Figure 16). With wry irony they turned to the same architectural firm—DeLemos and Cordes—that had designed Henry Siegel's own store. They had the architects create an open arcade lined with show windows to connect Broadway with 34th Street, thereby conveniently cutting the corner for pedestrians and assuring that the reduced

15 The Macy's corner in 1898 with the original holdout building sporting a bold billboard advertising the name of Siegel-Cooper, the rival department store that bought the little structure as an attempted manipulation against the giant retailer. *(Herbert Photos, courtesy of* Real Estate Forum*)*

16 The new Macy's store under construction at Herald Square. The original three-story holdout building at the 34th Street corner was distinctive even then for its use as a support for advertising signs. *(Irving Underhill, collection of Seymour Durst)*

17

18

17 An early advertising picture of Macy's showing an artist's conception of the original three-story holdout building without its advertising signs. *(R. H. Macy & Company)*

18 Macy's and the original holdout with its billboards. Saks & Company is at the left. *(Byron, courtesy of the Museum of the City of New York)*

street traffic in front of the corner building would reduce its value to Siegel. This public arcade remained for many years, until business growth dictated that it be converted to conventional selling space (Figures 17 and 18).

Despite the Macy's arcade around the corner building, the increased retail trade created by both Macy's and the new Saks and Company store on the south side of 34th Street increased the value of the holdout corner plot. Shortly after the two stores opened, the United Cigar Store Company leased the site for $40,000 per year and razed the original three-story building Mr. Smith had bought from Dr. Pell. In its place they built a more profitable five-story one, renting the ground floor to a restaurant and the upper stories to several businesses (Figure 19). During this process, for a very brief period there was the tantilizing sight of a vacant plot of land

on the corner, raising speculation that Macy's would at last be able to complete its building. The idea of such a scenario was quickly squelched, however, when a sign went up telling of the space for rent in the new building (Figure 20).

As for the defeated Henry Siegel, he was not much more successful at retailing than he had been at attempting to outwit Macy's. In 1902 his store on Sixth Avenue was bought out by the J. B. Greenhut Company, and in 1907 he sold the old Pell property back to Pop Smith for $500,000. Mr. Smith held the deed until 1911, when he sold it for $1,000,000.

Even with Mr. Siegel out of the way, however, Macy's still had corner problems. As the new building progressed, the Strauses decided to acquire the western half of the block earlier than planned. But in a replay of the embroglio with the southeast corner of the block,

19 Macy's in 1909 with the newly erected five-story corner building that replaced the original holdout. *(Detroit Publishing Company, collection of Seymour Durst)*

the owners of the northwest corner also refused to cooperate. The 23-foot by 60-foot building at 35th Street and Seventh Avenue was also needed, but its owners were not interested in selling—not even when the offer Macy's made was far in excess of the fair value of the little building and the land it occupied. Later, in 1926, Macy's demolished the numerous buildings occupying the western half of the block and erected a huge addition to its original building. The plans drawn by architect William Lawrence Bottomley provided a significant increase in selling space for the store, but the little corner holdout remained, forcing a notch to be cut into the 35th Street corner of the new structure (Figure 21).

The 35th Street building never became part of Macy's, and the 34th Street corner houses a Nedick's fast-food store, but fate (and some hard bargaining) has turned the hotdog-and-orange-drink counter into a support for a huge sign on its roof advertising the world's largest department store (Figure 22).

21

21 The later holdout against Macy's westward expansion at the southeast corner of 35th Street and Seventh Avenue. *(Andrew Alpern)*

22 The corner holdout transformed into a fast-food store and a giant advertising sign. (The New York Daily News)

22

20   HOLDOUTS

The Marbridge Building at Herald Square

Perhaps in emulation of the holdout thorn in Macy's side, a holdout situation developed directly across Herald Square in 1909, not long after the great store opened on 34th Street (Figure 23). William R. H. Martin bought the venerable brownstone Broadway Tabernacle Church on the corner of 34th Street and Sixth Avenue along with several other buildings, using a $3 million personal loan obtained from the drygoods merchant Benjamin Altman. He assembled a 200-foot by 150-foot site for his new eleven-story Marbridge Building—all except for an 18-foot-wide five-story brownstone at 76 West 35th Street whose owner would not sell.

76 West 35th Street The holdout structure had been built in 1881 by Thomas F. Carr. Henry McAleenan leased it from Mr. Carr, and after the owner's death in 1894, continued to lease it from his estate. In 1901 he bought the building, holding it against the attempts by developer Mr. Martin to buy it from him. Almost by way of a final act of defiance against Mr. Martin's huge new office building, Mr. McAleenan deeded his little holdout in 1911 to his six children, who kept it in the family at least until after World War II. The holdout remains, and the Marbridge Building stands today with a notch cut out of its northwest corner, testament to the obdurateness of its owner seventy-five years ago (Figure 24).

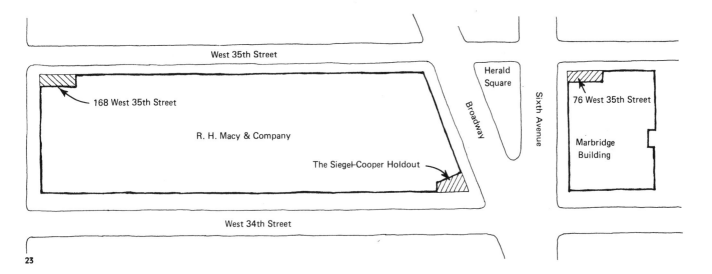

23

24

23 The holdouts against the Macy's and Marbridge buildings.

24 The Marbridge Building across Herald Square from Macy's showing its own holdout at 76 West 35th Street. *(Andrew Alpern)*

R.H. Macy & Company on Queens Boulevard

Something there is about the relationship between New York City and the department store founded by Rowland Husey Macy that seems to foster holdouts whenever real estate and construction are involved. In 1902 the store was forced to build around a holdout at the corner of 34th Street and Broadway. Later, the corner of 35th Street and Seventh Avenue stood fast against the store's westward expansion. And more recently, the acquisition of the corner property at Queens Boulevard and 55th Avenue proved unattainable when Macy's assembled the land for its store in the Elmhurst section of Queens.

In 1963 increased residential development in Queens led to the decision by Macy's to open its second branch store in that borough. It purchased about five acres of land on the north side of Queens Boulevard and planned a huge circular building in which five levels of parking facilities ringed a central core of selling space. Jack Green, a local realtor, had successfully negotiated on behalf of Macy's for all but the lot at the 55th Avenue corner, but he ran into an immovable opponent when he met its owner (Figure 25).

The architectural firm of Skidmore, Owings & Merrill had designed the new Macy's as a 426-foot-diameter concrete structure and planned a landscaped plaza at the corner. To accomplish this, the corner lot was needed, but Mrs. Mary Sendek, who lived there, didn't want to sell. When Broker Green couldn't budge the woman, Macy's vice president for real estate, Charles Cronheim, entered the picture.

Mary Sendek

Mr. Cronheim was up against a long-time resident. Joseph and Mary Sendek bought the little 20-foot by 30-foot frame house along with its 169-foot-deep lot for $4000 in 1922. It was an ordinary house, but in it she raised a family, and after her children had left and her husband had died, she continued to tend her backyard garden and maintain a run for her dog so he could exercise every day. The house represented forty years of Mrs. Sendek's life and she wasn't ready to part with it.

Mr. Cronheim recalled the efforts made to end the impasse. "We asked her to name a price," he said,

and she refused. She then suggested that we name a figure, and we did, far above what it was worth. After a long delay she said she didn't want to sell. Step by step we changed our offer. Instead of buying all the property we asked for only the back corner of it, a piece seven feet by fourteen feet, so we could complete our circular building. Then we asked for the air rights only, promising not to disturb her backyard. First she told us she liked to garden. Another time she said she didn't want to restrict her dog's play area. We went to five times the true value of the property without getting her to change her mind.

Mr. Cronheim tried on numerous occasions to win the woman over. He offered to buy her a new home in any part of the country, to move her at the store's expense, and then to give her enough more so that she would be well ahead of the game. But still she refused. Defeated, Mr. Cronheim instructed his architects to revise their plans.

The most practical way to do this was to eliminate the landscaped plaza and to cut a notch into the side of the building so it could avoid encroaching on the Sendek property. The architectural changes cost only $50,000. Mrs. Sendek had been offered $200,000 for her land, and the cost of building the plaza would not have been insignificant, so the holdout actually saved Macy's some money. But more to the point, it forced the store to occupy only a portion of the blockfront and denied it the grand entrance plaza that had been planned, thus detracting from the public's perception of the new building (Figure 26).

Mrs. Sendek died in 1980 and her estate sold the property to a local developer for $280,000 as the site for a small commercial building. Although the value of her estate could have been much larger had Mrs. Sendek accepted the Macy's offer, her son Victor put it succinctly when he said, "The house was my mother's life and we kept it for her."

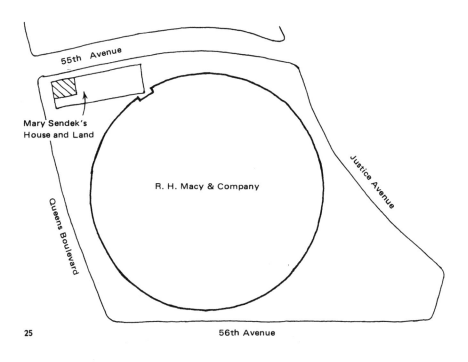

55th Avenue

Mary Sendek's
House and Land

Queens Boulevard

R. H. Macy & Company

Justice Avenue

56th Avenue

25

25 The Macy's store in Queens and the holdout.

26 Mrs. Sendek's incongruous holdout. The notch in Macy's circular building caused by the intruding back corner of her lot can clearly be seen by the discontinuity in the pattern of the windows in the Macy's structure toward the left side of the picture. (The New York Daily News)

26

3 East 83rd Street

27 The strangely out-of-place house at 3 East 83rd Street and its adjoining vacant lot in the late 1920s. The "For Sale" sign is deceptive; the figure of 32,795 square feet does not refer just to the single piece of unbuilt land but rather to all the Constable holdings on the block that were eventually demolished to make room for 1025 Fifth Avenue. *(von Urban, courtesy of the Museum of the City of New York)*

Perhaps the most charming holdout in all of Manhattan was the tiny two-story frame house that survived until 1953 at 3 East 83rd Street. Covered in white clapboards and sporting a front porch and wooden balustrades, the little building was a quaint anachronism overshadowed (but never overpowered) by the huge apartment houses that dominated its neighborhood (Figure 27).

The entire block on which the house stood was sold by the City of New York to John Graham in 1836 who sold the building lots individually, several being bought in 1851 by Thomas Pearson. Among these was the lot at 3 East 83rd Street, on which the little white house was erected some time between 1853 and 1867. Following the financial panic of 1873, Richard Arnold acquired a large portion of the 83rd Street block, including the white frame house. He erected a row of elegant brownstone houses on part of his holdings and a lavish mansion for himself, fronting on Fifth Avenue. Curiously however, he left undisturbed the little house and its adjoining lot to serve, perhaps inadvertently, as a buffer between his own home and the others he had built (Figure 28).

Richard Arnold was the son of Aaron Arnold who had founded a drygoods firm in 1825. In 1842 the elder Arnold's son-in-law James Constable joined him as partner to form the firm of Arnold, Constable & Company. Later, Richard's son, Hicks Arnold, also married a Constable—Harriet Matilda Constable—and they moved into the 83rd Street brownstone nearest the little white oddity. Hicks Arnold inherited the small house, and on his death in 1903 it passed to his wife. She continued to live in the larger stone house at number 7 while renting out the smaller structure. From 1913 to 1927 it was occupied by two sisters, the Misses Frances and Jennie Morris (Figures 29 and 30).

28

28 The house at East 83rd Street adjoining Richard Arnold's spacious home at the corner of Fifth Avenue, c. 1910. *(Collection of Andrew Alpern)*

29 The interior of 3 East 83rd Street during its occupancy by Frances and Jennie Morris, 1913–1927. *(Courtesy of the Museum of the City of New York)*

30 The interior of 3 East 83rd Street during its occupancy by Frances and Jennie Morris, 1913–1927. *(Courtesy of the Museum of the City of New York)*

29

30

1020 Fifth Avenue Encounters an Obstacle

In 1924, Michael Paterno bought Richard Arnold's former home at 1020 Fifth Avenue and razed it to make room for a luxury cooperative apartment house (Figure 31). He attempted to buy the diminutive home of the two sisters to give him the possibility of a larger structure, but Mrs. Arnold wouldn't hear of the two older women being forced out. To his credit, Mr. Paterno not only accepted the holdout graciously, he even altered his construction methods when the excavation blasting frightened the Morris sisters and broke some of their windowpanes.

Following the demise of one sister and the relocation of the other to Connecticut in 1929, Mrs. Hicks Arnold transferred ownership of the little house as well as much of the remaining property on both the 83rd Street and 84th Street frontages of the block to her relative, Edith Constable MacCracken, who herself lived at 15 East 83rd Street. The little house then had a succession of rental tenants over the years, but ownership of the house and the other midblock holdings remained in the Constable/Arnold family until 1953 when they were bought by N. K. Winston/ Holzer Associates. The company also acquired the 40-foot-wide former Frederick W. Vanderbilt house to provide a Fifth Avenue address for the side-street plottage. The developer then destroyed the existing houses and erected a pair of bleak apartment houses fronting on 83rd and 84th Streets, connected to a tasteless and seldom used ceremonial entrance at 1025 Fifth Avenue on the site of the Vanderbilt house (Figure 32).

Arnold, Constable & Company had for many years occupied a large store at 40th Street and Fifth Avenue on the site of an earlier home of Frederick W. Vanderbilt. While the Arnold family's little white frame house at 3 East 83rd Street held out for perhaps a hundred years, Arnold, Constable & Company lasted until its 150th birthday, closing its Fifth Avenue store finally in 1975.

31

31 1020 Fifth Avenue with the diminutive 3 East 83rd Street to the right and the former home of Frederick Vanderbilt to the left. *(Wurts, courtesy of the Museum of the City of New York)*

32 The ceremonial entrance to 1025 Fifth Avenue on the site of Frederick Vanderbilt's house. The two sections of 1025 are actually side-street buildings. The north portion can be seen in the background directly to the left of the lamppost; the south portion was erected in part on the site of the little frame holdout at 3 East 83rd Street. *(Andrew Alpern)*

32

1129 Broadway

About 1850, several large tracts of land in the vicinity of Madison Square were subdivided and sold, precipitating a modest construction boom in the area. Trinity Church began the erection of a large chapel on West 25th Street in 1851, completing it five years later. (The building still exists as the home of a Serbian congregation.) Around the corner on Broadway, two substantial brownstone-fronted residences were constructed, and at the 25th Street corner a five-story brick hostelry was built, christened the Worth House in recognition of the mortuary monument raised in 1857 across the street as a tomb and memorial to Major-General William Jenkins Worth who fought in the war with Mexico (Figure 33). Completing the westerly Broadway blockfront at 26th Street in 1866, the St. James Hotel was built as a grand, marble-fronted, six-story pile (Figure 34). Elegant retail establishments were opened to serve this substantial and affluent neighborhood.

As the nineteenth century wore on, commercial interests moved further and further north, particularly along the avenues. Gradually, the domestic character of the neighborhood began to change. Astute building owners recognized this and adapted to the changing conditions. The Townsend family had been one of the earliest lot buyers when the area was first developed. Faced with the declining receipts from its hotel at 25th Street, the family decided to replace it with an office building. To enlarge their plot, the family members acquired the small townhouse to the west of Worth House as well as one of the pair of brownstones on Broadway. The other, adjoining the St. James Hotel, refused to sell. Accepting the plot they then had as the largest that could be conveniently assembled, the family retained architect Cyrus L. W. Eidlitz (who later designed the Times Tower on Times Square) to plan an elegant twelve-story structure completely faced in limestone. The building was finished in 1896 and was named the Townsend Building.

That same year, Joseph and Abraham Pennock, builders from Philadelphia, bought the 30-year-old St. James Hotel for $1,025,000. They too attempted to buy the remaining brownstone at 1129 Broadway but were rebuffed. Following the example of the Townsend family, the Pennocks hired a well-known architect—Bruce Price—to design their own sixteen-story office structure known as the St. James Building. It was completed in 1897 (Figure 35).

The financial panic of 1907 brought disaster to many real estate investors, and in its wake, the Pittsburgh Life and Trust Company acquired title to the St. James

33

34

35

33 Broadway from Madison Square about 1890. The obelisk erected to the memory of Major-General William Jenkins Worth is at the extreme right. Opposite it at the corner of 25th street is the Worth House, razed a short time later for the Townsend Building. The St. James Hotel is at 26th Street. *(Courtesy of The New-York Historical Society)*

34 An early advertising view of the St. James Hotel. The artist has taken liberties with the architecture, showing an extra two-window bay at the left end of the building on the site of the adjacent brownstone. The brownstone never sold to the hotel, and it couldn't be bought for the successor St. James office building either. *(Courtesy of the Museum of the City of New York)*

35 Broadway at Madison Square in 1899. The tallest structure is the St. James Building at 26th Street. At the southern end of that block is the slightly lower Townsend Building and between them is the original five-story holdout building. *(J. S. Johnston, courtesy of the Museum of the City of New York)*

Building. The following year the company bought the former holdout at 1129 Broadway from the estate of Edward T. King, who had built the one-time residence and whose family had previously refused to sell it. Curiously, although there was apparently nothing wrong with the five-story brownstone, the company immediately demolished it, replacing the building with a one-story store. The structure survives today in that state (Figure 36).

36 The Townsend and St. James Buildings separated by a one-story holdout on the site of the original five-story holdout, c. 1910. *(Collection of Andrew Alpern)*

One Liberty Plaza

In 1967 the United States Steel Corporation and the Galbreath-Ruffin Corporation began planning for a 54-story office tower at Broadway and Liberty Street. Known as One Liberty Plaza and completed in 1972, the building was erected as the New York offices for U.S. Steel, with the remaining space rented to other companies (Figure 37).

In order to build a larger and more profitable structure, the developers obtained from the City Planning Commission in March 1968 an agreement permitting them to treat the two city blocks they owned as if they were one. The north block is bounded by Church, Liberty, and Cortlandt Streets, and by Broadway. The south block is bounded by Cedar and Liberty Streets, by Broadway, and by Trinity Place, the continuation of Church Street. The south block had originally been bisected by Temple Street, but this short and useless lane was closed and made part of the developer's holdings.

The agreement with the Planning Commission enabled a single building containing 1.8 million square feet to be erected on the north block. Without the special dispensation, the north block would have been restricted to a 1.3-million-square-foot building with a separate 500,000-square-foot structure on the south block.

37 An artist's rendering of One Liberty Plaza showing the holdout building housing Chock full o' Nuts at the right. (*Courtesy of Galbreath-Ruffin Corporation*)

The only fly in the ointment came in the form of two holdout buildings on the south block (Figure 38). The first of these, McCoys Restaurant at 139 Broadway was not considered to be a problem, since its lease expired on December 31, 1971—just about the time the U.S. Steel Building was expected to be completed. Ironically, the narrow, midblock, three-story McCoy building had been a holdout seventy years earlier against the developers of the two tall office buildings on either side of it. At that time it was the elegant classically designed home of the Liberty National Bank, a financial institution that boasted of assets of $3.6 million (Figure 39).

38 Broadway at Cedar Street. Number 139 in the center was a holdout at the beginning of the century when it house the Liberty National Bank. Occupied by McCoy's Restaurant it was again a holdout in 1967. Number 135 at the left was demolished down to its second floor in 1969 but the lower portion hung on for another ten years. *(Collection of Andrew Alpern)*

39 The Liberty National Bank at 139 Broadway at the turn of the century. A holdout in its own right, its building was later used by McCoy's Restaurant which briefly held out against the development of the extended site of One Liberty Plaza. *(Collection of Andrew Alpern)*

The real holdout problem was the Chock full o' Nuts store at 135 Broadway. It was 1967 and the famous counter restaurant held a lease that would tie up the property until 1980. While the Chock full o' Nuts building was no direct obstacle to the erection of One Liberty Plaza, it prevented the south block from being cleared entirely. Since the size of the building on the north block was conditioned on the complete south block being devoted to a park, the refusal of Chock full o' Nuts to relocate might prevent U.S. Steel from creating as large a building as they planned (Figure 40).

Several alternatives were presented to William Black, head of the restaurant chain he had founded in 1926. The first was for Chock full o' Nuts to move south across Cedar Street to 115 Broadway. Since space could not be provided for a ground floor store with access directly from the street, this proposal was rejected.

Space was then offered to Mr. Black for a new store on the concourse level of the new building U.S. Steel was going to build. Citing the $800,000 annual gross income from his restaurant, and noting that it was the second most profitable unit in his chain, Black completely rejected the concept of his relocating to basement space, which he felt would jeopardize his future profitability.

A cash payment of $1 million was then offered, but it too was rejected. This left the developers with the prospect of having a significant portion of the south block encumbered by the Chock full o' Nuts leasehold for thirteen years. Since the development of the north block to the desired building size was so dependent on the south block's new park, the dilemma left the builders perplexed.

Fortunately, the Planning Commission was especially farsighted and decided that a good thing was worth waiting for. It agreed to permit U.S. Steel to have the building it wanted on condition that 139 Broadway be demolished as soon as McCoys moved out at the end of 1971, that 135 Broadway be reduced at once to two stories in height, and that it be razed at the end of the Chock full o' Nuts' lease. Then—thirteen years after its beginning—the public park would be completed (Figure 41).

This scenario was played out, and in 1980 the Chock full o' Nuts 135 Broadway store was no more . . . and William Black had little in his pocket to show for it.

40

40 The Chock full o' Nuts store that held out for thirteen years against a public park. *(Courtesy of Chock full o' Nuts)*

41 The two holdout structures at Broadway and Cedar Street during the construction of One Liberty Plaza. *(David McLane and* The New York Sunday News*)*

41

80 Lafayette
Street

Rockefeller Center

While there is no physical evidence today for the passer-by to see, the roots of Rockefeller Center lie in the needs of grand opera. In January of 1926, financier and opera lover Otto H. Kahn was authorized by the Metropolitan Opera to seek a site for a new opera house to replace the ageing and inadequate building at 39th Street and Broadway. Numerous possibilities were investigated and several alternative architectural plans were developed, but for one reason or another all were rejected.

Then in January 1928, the broker responsible for maintaining the leases on the three midtown blocks owned by Columbia University suggested to the opera group that it build its new hall on a portion of one of the Columbia blocks. The location seemed appropriate to Mr. Kahn and his colleagues, so it was investigated. Their architect—with the image of the Paris Opera in his mind—declared that the site was too small for a suitably grand edifice. But the more grand the building and its setting, the more expensive its construction and its upkeep. It was quickly evident that for the opera house project to succeed, the remainder of the Columbia land would also have to be developed, with structures that could generate significantly greater profit than the long rows of brownstones and converted residences that then existed on the site.

In May 1928, a development plan for all the Columbia property was presented to a group headed by John D. Rockefeller, Jr. It surrounded a new opera house with arcades, plazas, and several income-producing buildings. Mr. Rockefeller thought the concept had merit so he made several economic studies to determine its viability. He then negotiated a lease with Columbia for the entire property, signing it on September 6, 1928.

Hiring his own team of architects, Mr. Rockefeller had scheme after scheme drawn, always with the opera house as the focal point. By mid-1929, the plan showed the central plaza and prome-

43 Four holdouts against the Rockefeller Center development.

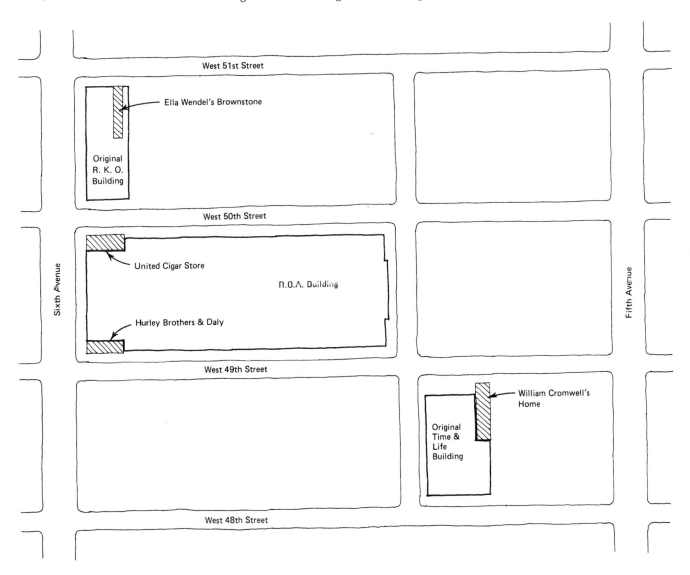

nade joining it to Fifth Avenue in a manner similar to the arrangement that was finally built. Surrounding the opera house were a hotel, an apartment-hotel, and buildings labeled "loft or apartment house."

In October 1929 the stock market crashed, and on December 3, the opera company backed out. Left with his lease with Columbia and a large deficit from the development money he had already invested, Mr. Rockefeller instructed his architects to prepare a plan for a purely commercial venture that would produce a satisfactory return on the remaining capital to be invested. To do this, it was determined that the project should extend all the way to Sixth Avenue—about a hundred feet further than Columbia owned. During 1930 and 1931, the Rockefeller interests began to buy the properties at the Sixth Avenue side of the site, and to buy out the long-term leases on the Columbia land.

Although the general public knew what was happening, there were relatively few really stubborn problems. Several holdouts developed, however; most eventually succumbed, but two still remain (Figure 43).

Lawyer William Cromwell's Home William Nelson Cromwell was the senior partner of the prestigious old law firm of Sullivan and Cromwell. He carried significant weight in the Republican party and was a loyal alumnus of Columbia University. He and his wife lived at 12 West 49th Street on a lease from Columbia. In his seventies, and with no children, Cromwell wanted to live out his days in the house that had been his home for many years and on which he had spent large sums to mold it to his idea of comfort (Figure 44).

Columbia found itself in an exceedingly awkward position. It was bound by the terms of the agreement with Mr. Rockefeller to turn over the separate properties as soon as the leases ran out. But the university had reason to believe it would receive a handsome bequest from the childless attorney when he died and it wanted to do nothing to endanger this expected windfall. Mr. Rockefeller didn't want to risk a lawsuit to gain possession of the house, partly because friends said Cromwell was ready to use all eighty lawyers in his firm to fight against eviction. It never came to open warfare, however. Columbia's president, Nicholas Murray Butler, had a chat with the holdout attorney and a new lease

44 At the top of a rather majestic flight of steps was the entrance to William Nelson Cromwell's holdout home at 12 West 49th Street. It was a classic limestone reconstruction from the turn of the century of an earlier brownstone row house similar to the remaining ones next to it. To the right of Cromwell's house is One Rockefeller Plaza—the first Time & Life Building. *(H. Barreuther, courtesy of The New-York Historical Society)*

was written, extending to 1948. When that one expired, Cromwell was 94 years old and no one wanted to force him out of his home. A few months later he himself expired, and the house was finally vacated. When the wrecking crew dismantled the building, they found hundreds of bottles of champagne in the cellar. The old lawyer had been known as a connoisseur of fine wines and the laborers opened a few magnums with gleeful anticipation. To their chagrin, every one had turned to vinegar.

The Last Wendel Ella Von Echtzel Wendel was born in 1853, and since 1856 she had lived in a stolid and lugubrious house on the northwest corner of 39th Street and Fifth Avenue. Her father, John Daniel Wendel, had built a sizable fortune—most of it in New York City real estate. When he died in 1876, his son and his seven daughters continued to invest prudently in land. They leased and developed, but they never sold what they bought. Practically all of the children refrained from marrying, devoting their energies to business. Their single-minded ability to generate money may have been hereditary, their grandfather having married a sister of the first John Jacob Astor. Ella Wendel was the last survivor of the family, living with her servants in the Fifth Avenue house that had been converted from gas lighting to electricity only a few years earlier. She was a difficult woman with whom to do business, since she saw no reason to have telephone service in her home. Accepting these obstacles, the Rockefeller interests attempted to purchase from her the house she owned at 70 West 51st Street, adjoining the Columbia property (Figure 45). Plying her with sweet words rather than hard business terms, the agents finally convinced Miss Wendel to lease her property for a period concurrent with the Columbia lease. The agreement didn't last long, however, since the venerable woman died on March 13, 1931, and her estate eventually sold the plot to Mr. Rockefeller.

Hurley's Saloon and the United Cigar Store More resistant than Ella Wendel were the two holdouts at the corners of the Sixth Avenue frontage that was to become the rear of the RCA Building. A plot 25 feet by 66 feet at 50th Street was occupied by a three-story building housing a United Cigar store, while a four-story structure on the 49th Street corner had its ground

45 The building at 70 West 51st Street that Ella V. Wendel was so reluctant to part with was an ordinary brownstone on a long block of almost identical buildings. While it was originally built as a one-family residence, it had long since ceased to function in that capacity. *(Roege, courtesy of the Museum of the City of New York)*

46

floor and basement under a long-term lease to three Irishmen: the brothers Hurley and Mr. Daly, who had formed a partnership in 1892 and opened a saloon (Figures 46, 47, and 48).

In 1804, Dr. David Hosack purchased the land later leased out by Columbia for Rockefeller Center. The east side of what is now Sixth Avenue from 49th Street to 50th Street was then part of the land of Andrew Hopper. Mr. Hopper's land fronted on Broadway, the grid of Manhattan's streets not having been laid out yet. Mr. Hopper's heirs subdivided his property after his death, and in 1852, a grocer named John F. Boronowsky bought the plot of land at what is now 74 West 50th Street, perhaps anticipating the extension of Sixth Avenue past his property, which was accomplished in 1856. He paid $1600 for the site and refused all offers to sell it. His daughter too held on to the property, as did his grandson, J. Fred Maxwell. Mr. Maxwell had leased the building that stood on his grandfather's land to the United Cigar Company for $16,000 a year, and he saw no reason to give it up to the Rockefeller agents. The cigar store was succeeded by a Whelan's drugstore, but it was not until 1962, after Mr. Max-

46   The east side of Sixth Avenue from 49th to 50th Streets in 1921. With the advent of prohibition, the Hurley Brothers & Daly saloon gave way to the shop in the picture selling flowers, but the underlying lease was retained by the tavern's owners . . . to the chagrin of the Rockefeller interests a decade later. The entire Rockefeller Center site was covered with buildings of this scale prior to 1930, most on land rented from Columbia University. *(Roege, courtesy of the Museum of the City of New York)*

47   The site of the RCA Building standing all but vacant in 1931. Visible beyond the tracks of the Sixth Avenue elevated is the United Cigar store's building at the 50th Street corner. At 49th Street is the four-story brick building under lease to the Messrs. Hurley and Daly. For many years the ground floor was occupied by a florist's establishment and a smoke shop, but following the repeal of prohibition, the Hurley Brothers & Daly saloon reopened its doors there. Today the spot is tenanted by an unrelated restaurant/bar called Hurley's. (The New York Times)

48 (a) & (b)   Seemingly held up by a pair of bookends, the Sixth Avenue end of 30 Rockefeller Plaza, known as 1250 Avenue of the Americas to tourists, is flanked to the south by Hurley's, and to the north by the building that formerly housed the United Cigar Store. *(Andrew Alpern)*

38   HOLDOUTS

47

48a

48b

well had died, that the ownership of the property passed out of the family. Sold by his widow for $380,000, the deed was acquired by Rockefeller Center in 1972. A Lindy's restaurant now occupies the considerably altered building.

There was no particular difficulty for the Rockefeller group to acquire title to the 49th Street building, but the Irishmen's lease prevented it from being demolished. The three men had the right of occupancy until 1942 and they refused to give it up unless they received $250,000—a sum Mr. Rockefeller was unwilling to pay. So the building stayed, and after the repeal of prohibition the Hurley Brothers & Daly saloon reopened, with the lease renewed annually after 1942. Eventually the tavern closed. The building was then extensively remodeled, altering it from a genuinely evolved nineteenth century saloon into a pseudo-nineteenth century eatery dubbed Dan Wolf's Steak and Seafood Restaurant. After less than two years under that moniker however, its proprietors restored the name of Hurley's, accepting the refusal of loyal New Yorkers to abandon the name of the brothers who stood up against the Rockefeller power . . . and won (or did they lose?). Just as no one but a tourist would refer to Sixth Avenue as the Avenue of the Americas—even after more than a quarter century of official name-change—some aspects of New York life seem to have a tenacity that defies description or obliteration. Holdouts aren't always physical.

Celanese Building

During the 1960s, Rockefeller Center expanded to the western side of Sixth Avenue and in partnership with several corporate giants built four tall office structures: the Time & Life Building, the Exxon Building, the McGraw-Hill Building, and the Celanese Building (Figure 49). The land for the most southerly of these, the Celanese Building at 1211 Sixth Avenue, was assembled gradually, with all land purchases completed by the end of 1967. Two residential tenants in buildings on the site held fast and refused to budge, however, thus preventing the completion of the demolition work and the commencement of the excavations for the new building (Figure 50).

Mr. "R" One, a Mr. "R.," was a writer living in a tiny apartment at 132 West 48th Street, a converted private row house of the 1870s. Mr. "R." was a statutory tenant insulated by the provisions of the New York City Rent Control law. His rent had originally been $100 per month, but instead of escalating in parallel with the relentless rise in the overall cost of living, it was reduced to $72 per month by the Rent Control Commission on his petition of alleged diminution of services (Figure 51).

This writer was working on a book which he expected someone to publish. He claimed that his only reason for refusing to move was his desire to finish his new book. But perhaps his true feelings were better reflected in a comment he made that was reported in *The New York Times* which suggested he relished the idea of holding up, "even for a few minutes, a giant proposition like this."

L. Reyner Samet was one of the lawyers representing the Rockefeller Center interests. He had negotiated successfully with many of the owners and tenants on the site, but after several frustrating months of fruitless talks with Mr. "R." he observed that it was a lot easier dealing with business people than with writers. Commenting on holdouts, he said, "When a fellow owns a building or has a lease there's not a damn thing we can do but pay. We have no condemnation power. It's just a matter of settling on a price."

49 The Celanese Building, where construction was delayed by two residential holdout tenants whose tiny apartments were in buildings already acquired by the Rockefeller development interests. The open plaza area faces Sixth Avenue between 47th and 48th Streets. *(Bo Parker, courtesy of Rockefeller Center, Inc.)*

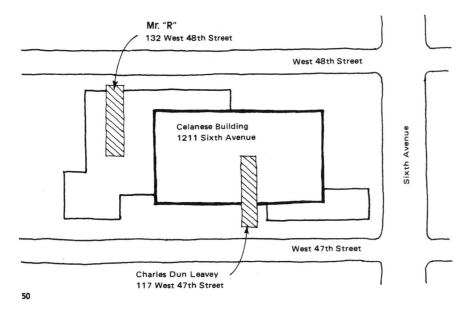

The price Mr. "R." finally agreed to was more than $20,000, $5000 of which was paid by the demolition contractor who was particularly anxious to bulldoze the building out of the way. Mr. "R." may have felt he had the last word when he said, after he had vacated the building, that the Rockefeller agents couldn't seem to understand why anyone would "hold up progress" just to write a book. So he chose to hold up progress.

Charles Dun Leavey Charles Dun Leavey also held up the progress of the Celanese Building for many months while he fought eviction at the Rent Control Commission. This New York State University doctoral candidate occupied a two-room apartment at 117 West 47th Street where he had been living for eleven years, paying $29.76 per month. At first he appeared to be enamored of the particular site, saying "All I want is an apartment in the new Celanese Building. That little building over there is as close to paradise as I've ever been, and I want to stay on the same piece of land." Later, however, he said that he had no intention of ever vacating and that he was "setting a good, pugnacious, stubborn example of social effectiveness, social usefulness for the needy, ignorant, insecure, helpless tenants throughout the city of New York." Ironically, Mr. Dun Leavey, who was ultimately defeated in his battle against Rockefeller Center, was once a recipient of a Rockefeller Foundation study grant.

50   The Celanese Building and the two holdouts.

51   The former brownstone at 132 West 48th Street in which Mr. "R." held out against the construction of the Celanese Building. He finally left his $72-per-month apartment in exchange for a cash payment of more than $20,000. (The New York Times)

770 Broadway

The massive block-square office building at 770 Broadway has a solid and finished appearance, but for the first twenty years of its existence it had a large chunk missing from its southwest corner.

The building was designed in 1903 as an expansion for the John Wanamaker store on the next block north. It was planned to look the way it does today, but Wanamaker's was unable to obtain possession of all the necessary land. The property is owned by Sailors' Snug Harbor, a refuge for "aged, decrepit and worn-out sailors" now located in North Carolina. Sailors' Snug Harbor was established in accordance with the terms of the will of Robert Randall, who died in 1801. The land he had left for the old sailors had originally been the farm bought by his father, Captain Thomas Randall. By the time the Randall estate was settled, more than twenty years after Robert Randall's death, the trustees appointed to set up the retirement community elected to build quarters for the old salts on Staten Island and to rent out the farm land on long-term leases.

In preparation for its expansion, Wanamaker's was able to buy up the leases for all of the smaller buildings on the block, but the cost of acquiring possession of the newly built large nine-story structure at the corner of Broadway and 8th Street was prohibitive (Figure 52). The new store was built around the holdout (Figure 53), and it remained in that unfinished state until 1926, when the leasehold was finally acquired and the store building completed (Figure 54). When Wanamaker's closed in 1954, its building at 770 Broadway was converted to offices.

A. T. Stewart's Store Ironically, the original Wanamaker store building a block further up Broadway had also suffered from a holdout. Its site was also part of the Randall farm and is owned by Sailors' Snug Harbor. In 1862, the pioneering drygoods merchant Alexander T. Stewart planned a relocation of his retail store from its original location at Chambers Street. Setting his sights on the entire Broadway block from 9th Street to 10th Street, he bought out the existing property leases ... except for the one for the small building near the corner of Broadway and 9th Street

52 The easterly blockfront of Broadway from 8th Street to 9th Street in 1899. The three buildings on the northern half of the block were demolished to make room for the new Wanamaker store but the leasehold for the nine-story structure at the right could not be bought and the building remained as a holdout. (*"A Pictorial Description of Broadway" as published by* The Mail & Express *newspaper*)

53 The building at 770 Broadway in 1910 with the nine-story holdout building at the right. Built as an expansion of the John Wanamaker store, the structure was connected by a bridge over 9th Street to the old A. T. Stewart store building which Mr. Wanamaker had acquired in 1896. *(Collection of Andrew Alpern)*

54 In 1926, 770 Broadway finally achieved this appearance. The removal of the holdout on the 8th Street corner enabled the architect's original design to be fulfilled—almost a quarter of a century after it had been prepared. *(Lloyd Acker, courtesy of The New York Public Library)*

occupied by the French art gallery of Goupil, Vibert & Company. The little store could not be budged, so Stewart built around it in anticipation of ultimately acquiring the site (Figure 55). When he finally did, it was an easy thing to expand his building, which had been constructed of cast iron components that simply bolted together.

In 1896, after Mr. Stewart's death, Mr. Wanamaker bought the store. That original building was destroyed by fire in 1956. The apartment building that replaced it is called Stewart House to perpetuate the name of the old merchant. The old sea captain and his son are memorialized in the name of another apartment structure nearby—Randall House. But the name of Goupil is totally forgotten, and the identity of the leaseholder who thwarted Mr. Wanamaker is not even known. A moral, perhaps?

55 The first Wanamaker building when it was still the A. T. Stewart store. This photograph was taken about 1869 and shows the missing corner of the building (later filled in) caused by the Goupil, Vibert & Company holdout. Tenth Street is at the left and Broadway at the right in this picture published by E. & H. T. Anthony & Co. *(Courtesy of Frederick S. Lightfoot)*

179 West Street

During the 1960s, New York City announced with great fanfare a redevelopment plan known as the Washington Street Project. Designed to rejuvenate a huge area adjoining the Hudson River north of what has since become the World Trade Center, the original scheme called for the total bulldozing of a twenty-five-block site. Title to all the buildings was acquired through condemnation and demolition proceeded rapidly. Plans for the reconstruction of the area bogged down, however, prompting one tenant to refuse to move until assured that something more promising than a vacant lot would be forthcoming from the razing of his workplace and home.

Mardig Kachian, a sculptor, occupied a four-room apartment plus a large studio in the four-story mid-nineteenth century building at 179 West Street, between Warren and Chambers Streets. When the building was the last one that remained standing on the site, the City went to court to evict the artist. But in 1970 a federal judge barred demolition of the structure, "until such time as projects planned for the renewal have been authorized by all appropriate governmental bodies and until such time as sponsors proceed forthwith with the development of the renewal site" (Figure 56).

The City had already cut off Mr. Kachian's water, but armed with the federal court's ruling, the sculptor went to State Supreme Court, which ordered the reconnection of this utility. The project took two weeks and cost several thousand dollars since an entirely new water line had to be run to the main, a new tap made, and the entire excavation refilled and the street resurfaced.

Mardig Kachian remained as a holdout, paying the City $75 a month in rent for his duplex accommodations. It was not until the 1980s that the renewal project was resurrected and recast to meet a new set of criteria. Only then, a decade and a half after the plans had first been announced, was the holdout building's fate sealed.

56 The lonesome form of 179 West Street in a bleak landscape of parking lots and weeds—a monument to one man's refusal to abandon his home to the wreckers until definite plans were ready for the redevelopment of the site. *(Andrew Alpern)*

London Terrace

57

57 The 1845 buildings of the London Terrace as they appeared late in the 19th century.

58 (a) & (b) Henry Mandel's massive London Terrace apartment development in 1983, and the original rental office in 1931.

58a

Perhaps the most difficult holdouts a developer can encounter are those cantankerous souls whose sole reason for refusing to move is the opportunity to attain a bit of notoriety and the chance to tilt in an otherwise pointless battle. Such was Tillie Hart, who replied to attempts at a negotiated settlement with the comment, "I'm not going to move. It's a matter of principle."

Tillie Hart Mrs. Hart occupied the three-story - and - basement rowhouse at 429 West 23rd Street under a sublease which she asserted was valid until May 1930. The underlying house lease had expired in May of 1929, however, and builder/developer Henry Mandel had negotiated his own long-term lease on the property. Mr. Mandel had similarly acquired possession of all the other buildings on the block-square site extending from Ninth Avenue to Tenth Avenue north of 23rd Street

(Figure 57). He planned to erect a massive apartment house complex and intended to call it London Terrace, after the 1845 row of townhouses of which Mrs. Hart's home formed a part. During the summer of 1929, Mr. Mandel worked on the clearing of the site and by October had razed all the existing structures except the one in which Mrs. Hart lived. He excavated all around the old structure and began pouring the concrete foundations for his new buildings while attempting to oust the woman from the house.

Mr. Mandel and his lawyers had been battling the woman for several months before the newspapers found the increasingly histrionic tactics of Mrs. Hart to be worthy of mention in print. On October 1, 1929, the first of a month-long series of articles appeared, documenting the repeated skirmishes between the beleaguered builder and the tenacious tenant. Mrs. Hart barricaded

herself inside the house along with her cousin Anthony Nugent and a boarder, Andrew Jackson. A succession of lawyers assisted her in warding off the legal maneuvers of the Mandel organization. Mr. Mandel got a court order; she obtained a stay; he secured a declaration from the Department of Buildings that the house was unsafe; she obtained another stay; he had an eviction order signed; she became ill.

Back and forth it went until October 20, when she was ordered to pay $600 in back rent or be forcibly evicted in five days. She then pleaded poverty and announced plans for a theatrical benefit performance to raise the necessary money. The performance was never held, and she couldn't come up with sufficient funds, so her belongings were taken out of the house and placed on the sidewalk on October 25. Obstinate to the last, Mrs. Hart spent that night sleeping in the house on newspapers spread out on the floor, but finally the following day she abandoned the fight and gave the house over to the wreckers who demolished it in short order.

Following the removal of Mrs. Hart from the site, and despite the calamitous events on Wall Street, construction proceeded rapidly on Mr. Mandel's new London Terrace. In December 1929 the cornerstone was laid, and perhaps in commemoration of Mrs. Hart's long fight, the stone was taken from the foundation of the house the woman had refused to leave. An inscription was carved into it asserting that it was "an original stone from the Clement Moore house which stood on this site." Mr. Mandel was stretching history a bit on that point, however, since the home in which the author of 'Twas the Night Before Christmas* lived had been located a block further south (Figure 58).

58D

Allerton House

The second half of the nineteenth century saw a proliferation of stables in the developing sections of Manhattan to accommodate the vast numbers of horses needed to pull the increasing numbers of commercial wagons and private carriages, as well as countless coaches, omnibuses, and hansom cabs. One of these was the Saratoga Stables, a four-story structure built about 1870 that fronted 75 feet on Lexington Avenue and extended 90 feet westward on the block between 56th Street and 57th Street. The north side of the building was separated from fashionable 57th Street by a 25-foot strip of land on which had been built four small brownstone-fronted, bay-windowed, high-stooped private houses.

Following World War I, the burgeoning use of cars and trucks to replace the less efficient horse-drawn vehicles rendered the city's stables fertile fields for real estate development. In 1920, in line with this trend, the Saratoga Stables site was bought for development as a residential hotel for single working women. Also purchased were three of the four residential buildings adjoining the stables along 57th Street.

698 Lexington Avenue The house at 698 Lexington Avenue on the corner could not be bought, however. Originally constructed for the Odell Estate about 1875, it had been leased as a one-family residence until 1900, when it was converted for use as apartments—one on each of its upper four floors plus a shop at the ground level. It then changed hands several times until Leo and Abraham Schwab sold it to Morris Blum in 1913.

When the hotel developers could not come to terms with Mr. Blum on a sale of the property, they instructed architect Arthur Loomis Harmon (whose firm later designed the Empire State Building) to plan the hotel around the corner holdout. Drawings were filed with the building department in May 1921 and

59a

in July demolition of the existing structures on the site began. Even with his little building standing in solitary isolation amid the excavation work, and then overshadowed by the progress of construction, Mr. Blum still refused to sell. In May 1922, however, he agreed to a long-term lease of his property to the Allerton Corporation. The lease document gave the hotel people the right to alter or enlarge Mr. Blum's building— or even to replace it with a completely new structure. But curiously, it was stipulated that at no time could the corner building be connected in any way with the adjoining hotel, and that it had to have its own heating system and internal stairway. The reasoning behind this strange agreement is hard to fathom. Mr. Blum was a real estate investor who by 1927 had acquired four other Lexington Avenue buildings. One would have thought that he might have made a better deal by selling his property outright to the Allerton developers. Perhaps he

was merely guilty of poor business judgment; his judgment wasn't very good in July of 1922 either, when he sold bootleg whiskey to undercover prohibition agents and was arrested for his pains.

Shortly after the developer acquired the corner building, architect Harmon filed plans to alter it, adding a sixth story and a distinctive roof cornice, and replacing the façade with one compatible with his design for the hotel. The construction work was done quickly, and the alteration was completed concurrent with the opening of the Allerton in the summer of 1923 (Figure 59). Occupancy of the little holdout was initially a combination of apartments and a small private club, but gradually the entire building became commercial. An elevator was added in 1938, but in accordance with the lease terms, the smaller building remained separate from the hotel. Ownership of the two structures did not converge until 1960, when Sol Goldman bought both.

The hotel remains a hotel—possibly to be converted to cooperative apartments if the rent stabilization laws governing hotel rooms are ever repealed— while the little building continues its commercial usage. Whatever Morris Blum's reasons were for keeping the two structures distinct from each other, their ongoing status in that condition doubtless keeps his ghost at rest.

59 (a) & (b) Looking south on Lexington Avenue to the corner of 57th Street. At the left is the scene in 1912 showing the Saratoga Stables on the avenue and the brownstones on 57th Street. Partially obscured by subway construction materials, the corner building shows its recent partial conversion to commercial uses. At the right is the same view almost half a century later. Allerton House at 130 East 57th Street wraps around the virtually unrecognizable corner brownstone. The top floor, heavy roof cornice, and compatible brick façade of the little building were added by the hotel owners after they took a long-term lease on the holdout structure. *(Left: courtesy of The New-York Historical Society; Right: Lloyd Acker, courtesy of The New York Public Library)*

59b

City Investing Building

The City Investing Building was located at 165 Broadway at Cortlandt Street until taken down to provide part of the site for the United States Steel Corporation's building at One Liberty Plaza (Figure 60). Elaborately ornamented in limestone, it was the object of a brief skirmish to preserve it in 1968 by those who felt that the statuary groups at the two main entrances were worth more to the city than the benefits that would accrue from the development of the two-block square site.

Built in 1908 by the Heddon Construction Company to the designs of Francis H. Kimball, the building contained more than half a million square feet in its thirty-four stories. It surrounded a much smaller six-story structure which held out at the corner of the block. Originally named for its builder, Peter Gilsey (whose Gilsey Hotel still stands at Broadway and 29th Street), the corner structure was renamed several times until being called the Wessells Building at the beginning of the twentieth century. This holdout was distinctive for its facade constructed completely of cast-iron elements fabricated in 1853 by Daniel D. Badger, whose

169 Broadway

60

Architectural Iron Works was responsible for many innovative cast-iron structures that still exist in New York City (Figure 61).

Less than a decade after the completion of the City Investing Building its owners were able to acquire the one-time holdout. They demolished it and erected in its place an addition to 165 Broadway more compatible in appearance to the taller structure. Gone now are 165 Broadway, its addition, and the old Gilsey Building, unremembered by all but the most dedicated architectural historians.

60 An early publicity view of the City Investing Building at 165 Broadway before the corner holdout was replaced with a compatible addition to its towering neighbor. *(Collection of Andrew Alpern)*

61 The 1853 cast-iron fronted building at Broadway and Cortlandt Street that held out against the giant City Investing Building, as it appeared in 1906. Originally known as the Gilsey Building, it had gone through several other names by the time this photograph was made. *(Irving Underhill, courtesy of the American Architectural Archive)*

61

Borden Building

Remnants of midtown Manhattan's residential past remained well into the twentieth century in the form of small brownstone-fronted buildings—some still occupied as one-family homes—along Madison Avenue and on the adjoining side streets. When the venerable clothing firm of Brooks Brothers celebrated its 100th anniversary in 1918 at its new "uptown" location at Madison Avenue and 44th Street, its ten-story building overshadowed its many small-scaled neighbors. Following Brooks's lead, the Borden Company decided to erect its own headquarters at the adjoining corner of 45th Street.

348 Madison Avenue Borden was able to acquire eight parcels, but two important ones eluded its grasp (Figure 62). One was a 22-foot-wide four-story house immediately adjacent to the Brooks Brothers building. Peter A. H. Jackson owned it until his death in 1895. His will stipulated that it was to be leased out with the income being divided among his children. After the deaths of all his children, the property was then to be divided among his grandchildren, including those as yet unborn at the time of his own demise. Following the terms of the will, his executors leased the house in 1902 to Thomas B. Hidden for a term of twenty-one years, with two 21-year renewal options. Since the Jackson estate would not consider a sale because of the interests of those as-yet-unborn grandchildren, Borden made no attempt to acquire Mr. Hidden's leasehold. However, when Mr. Hidden declined to exercise his renewal option in 1923, the year after 350 Madison Avenue had been completed, the Borden Company leased the little building from Mr. Jackson's executors.

24 East 45th Street The second holdout was a 30-foot-wide brownstone at 24 East 45th Street. It was the home of George F. Cornell and his family for many years and when Mr. Cornell died in 1898, his wife received the right to remain in residence as long as she wished . . . providing she did not remarry. As an added condition, she was required to provide lodging for their two daughters, should those two women wish to live there. Mrs. Agnes Cornell did not remarry, and she continued to live in the spacious old house, rejecting Borden's offers for it.

Despairing of budging Mrs. Cornell, Borden directed the architectural firm of Buchman & Kahn to design the office structure around the holdout. The result was an awkward and inefficient building, but perhaps the best that could have been expected under the circumstances (Figure 63). The construction project was made even more difficult,

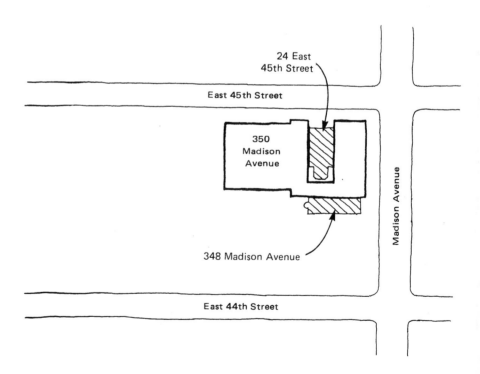

62 350 Madison Avenue with its holdouts.

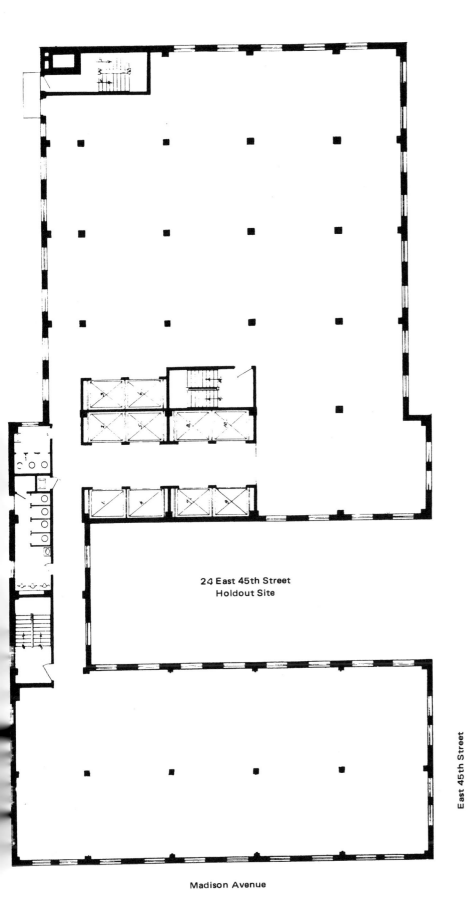

24 East 45th Street
Holdout Site

East 45th Street

Madison Avenue

63 The plan of a typical upper floor of 350 Madison Avenue as originally constructed. The courtyard on the 45th Street side surrounds one of the holdouts. Without that impediment, only two fire stairs would have been required instead of the three that are shown, and the floor plan could have been more effectively utilized by the building's tenants. The second holdout on the Madison Avenue side dictated that the entrance lobby be inappropriately small for the size of the building itself.

64 A photograph taken on February 1, 1921, during the construction of 350 Madison Avenue, then known as the Borden Building. At the corner, the Olivotti art gallery has erected a sign announcing its impending relocation to 72nd Street, but in the meantime it became a temporary holdout, delaying completion of the new office structure. *(Irving Underhill, courtesy of the Museum of the City of New York)*

65 The Borden Building at 350 Madison Avenue as originally constructed. The courtyard on 45th Street surrounded the holdout at number 24. *(Chester B. Price)*

however, by a short-term holdout in the form of the Olivotti art gallery, which occupied a former private house at the Madison Avenue corner. Olivotti was delayed in relocating to its new gallery at Madison and 72nd Street by its own construction problems, so it refused to vacate its 45th Street premises. This made it necessary for Borden to construct its office tower in sections, thereby increasing its costs (Figure 64). In 1922, 350 Madison Avenue was finally completed, and Borden moved in (Figure 65).

Only two years later, on February 6, 1924, Mrs. Cornell died. Her daughter Anna Brinley worked quickly to settle the estate, and on April 23 of that year, sold her erstwhile family home to Borden. The company demolished it and extended the lower three floors of its own building to fill the site of George Cornell's old house (Figure 66).

Ultimately, Borden acquired ownership of the Jackson holdout it had been leasing, and in 1967 tore it down. In its place the company built a grandiose new entrance to its building, replacing the small side-street lobby (Figure 67). Not long after, however, Borden decided to leave New York City. It sold its building to the Condé Nast magazine publishing company, which planned a major renovation to the old structure. Perhaps most significant, the courtyard that the original architects had been forced to construct on the 45th Street side to avoid the holdout building was finally completely filled in, giving 350 Madison Avenue the simple rectangular form the Borden Company had wanted in the beginning. The building was finished and occupied by Condé Nast in 1972, fulfilling the design scheme drawn more than fifty years before.

66 350 Madison Avenue in 1968 following the creation of a new avenue entrance on the site of one of the original holdouts. The open court in the middle of the side street elevation indicates the position of the other holdout. *(Lloyd Acker, courtesy of The New York Public Library)*

67 The front of 350 Madison Avenue showing the grandiose entrance that was constructed when the old holdout brownstone was bought and demolished. *(Andrew Alpern)*

66

67

Citibank Building

Usually, when a property owner holds out for an unreasonable price or an unacceptable demand and the developer decides to build around him, an opportunity is lost forever, and the holdout is left with property greatly diminished in value. But this is not always the case. For Jacob A. Michels, it paid to hold out for more than five years, long past the apparent point of no return.

Early in 1953, Vincent Astor began to assemble the entire block bounded by Lexington and Park Avenues and 53rd and 54th Streets for a project to be known as Astor Plaza (Figure 68). One by one he reached agreement with nineteen of the twenty property owners, paying about $8,000,000 for the land. He also spent $500,000 and countless

68 399 Park Avenue as envisioned by Vincent Astor. Its appearance remained unchanged when actually constructed as the headquarters building for the First National City Bank. *(Collection of Seymour Durst)*

68

hours of negotiation to buy out the leases of about 250 commercial and residential tenants.

Michels Pharmacy Jacob A. Michels owned the final holdout—a five-story walkup building at 620 Lexington Avenue with a drugtore on the ground floor run by Mr. and Mrs. Michels (Figure 69). Mr. Astor's offer for the property escalated steadily until a final limit of $400,000 was reached. But still Mr. Michels would not sell. Mrs. Michels was quoted as saying, "They think that because they're the Astors they can wave a magic wand and everyone does what they want. But they can't go around driving little people out of business."

Despairing of ever acquiring the Michels' property at a realistic price, Mr. Astor had his building redesigned so it would sit on its site in such a way as to enable him to build around the 20-foot by 68-foot holdout (Figure 70). Demolition proceeded all around the drugstore building and the excavation work was begun.

But then Mr. Astor ran into financing difficulties which he could not surmount, so he abandoned the project to the First National City Bank, now known as Citibank. That practical institution did not wish to prolong or complicate the building process, so it paid Mr. Michels the price he had demanded, and in addition gave him a choice of new sites for his store. Mr. Michels emerged from the battle considerably richer—and with a new drugstore to boot. And Citibank got its building . . . offset on the site almost in commemoration of the holdout. Only Mr. Astor suffered, but perhaps he had overextended himself and would have come to grief even without the problem of Mr. Michels. Who can tell?

69

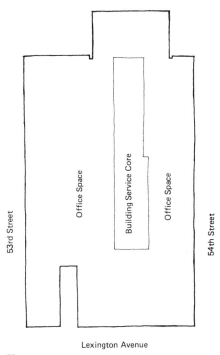

70

69 The anomalous structure on Lexington Avenue in 1958 when the remainder of the block-square building site was owned by Vincent Astor. The excavation had begun to the north of the little holdout, but before the new tower was erected, the site changed hands, Mr. Michels's drugstore was purchased, and the nineteenth-century pile reduced to rubble. *(Neal Boenzi and* The New York Times*)*

70 A typical lower floor as planned for Astor Plaza at 399 Park Avenue. The notch at the bottom of the plan was necessary to accommodate Jacob Michels's holdout on Lexington Avenue. When the First National City Bank took over the project and bought out Mr. Michels, the notch was no longer needed and the building was completed in a more conventional form.

201 East 42nd Street

The often multilayered nature of New York City real estate ownership and control can play havoc with a developer who wants to acquire a particular piece of property. An excellent example of this stands as mute testimony to the unreasonable demands of three layers of control of 679 Third Avenue at the southeast corner of 43rd Street. A rather seedy looking relic that dates from the time of the construction of the long-defunct Third Avenue elevated railway, the five-story wood and brick structure is overwhelmed by the adjacent thirty-one-story office tower against which it is a holdout (Figure 71).

In 1944, The Durst Organization bought the twenty-one-story office building at 205 East 42nd Street. Known as the Bartholomew Building, it had been built in the late 1920s on the site of the Parish House of St. Bartholomew's Church. Along with the office building came ownership of two small buildings adjoining on Third Avenue to act as light protectors, since presumably without these two parcels a developer would not be able to erect a building capable of blocking the light from the windows on the west face of number 205. Also part of the deal was a leasehold on a two-story building at the 42nd Street corner of the avenue. With that building operating at a loss, the Dursts let the lease lapse, whereupon it was picked up by William Zeckendorf who promptly announced plans to erect his own twenty-one-story office building on the 60-foot by 80-foot plot. Financing realities couldn't fulfill the concept, however, and Mr. Zeckendorf gave the lease back to the Durst interests.

By that time, in 1961, office usage had changed, making the maintenance of light and views at the westerly windows of 205 East 42nd Street much less important. Recognizing this, the Durst family decided to improve the entire Third Avenue blockfront from 42nd Street to 43rd Street with a new office tower. It quickly acquired all but one of the remaining parcels of land needed

679 Third Avenue for the new building. That one, at the 43rd Street end of the block, had been leased in its entirety by its owner to a man who in turn had subleased the ground floor tavern for a lengthy term. That made three levels of control that would have to be bought out before the building could be demolished. Each of these controlling interests thought he held the trump card, and each demanded what

71

72

he thought to be a suitable price. When these costs were totaled, the acquisition of the final three percent of the site would have added fifty percent to the price of the remainder of the land.

The Dursts felt that this was completely out of proportion, so they left the old building where it was (Figure 72), and built their new one around it, completing the project in 1965 (Figure 73). Years later, they had an opportunity to acquire the holdout building at a more realistic price, but the owner reneged at the last minute and sold it to someone else. Had The Durst Organization bought the old structure, it would have been razed and the office building extended. Instead, the new owner demanded increasingly high rentals for the ground floor store, resulting in a succession of tenants. Instead of stability and architectural consistency at 43rd Street, there is visual cacophony and continual change. And all because of a holdout.

71 The century-old structure at 679 Third Avenue that prevented 201 East 42nd Street from extending the full blockfront to 43rd Street. *(Andrew Alpern)*

72 The site of 201 East 42nd Street during excavation work. The construction digging surrounds the little five-story holdout building. *(Courtesy of* Real Estate Forum*)*

73 A view of 201 East 42nd Street with the holdout building partially hidden at the left. To the right is the Bartholomew Building, now called the Conover-Mast Building. *(Lew Rosen, courtesy of The Durst Organization)*

73

Lorillard Building

Mere property ownership doesn't necessarily guarantee a developer the land needed for a new building. Tenants holding long-term leases can also stand in the way of progress.

During the 1950s, Seymour Durst assembled a plot of land 100 feet by 200 feet in order to construct a large office building to be known as the Lorillard Building. He owned all the property on the east side of Third Avenue from 41st Street to 42nd Street (Figure 74), including a five-story loft building at 202 East 42nd Street. The ground floor of that structure, however, was occupied by a Rudley's Coffee Shop on a lease that ran until 1970. Negotiations with the management of the Rudley's chain proved fruitless, the restaurateurs holding out for a price far in excess of a reasonable figure.

Rudley's Coffee Shop

Rather than letting his property lie fallow until 1970, Durst built his twenty-seven-story office building anyhow, leaving a notch in the corner for the Rudley's building (Figures 75 and 76). The new structure was completed in 1958, and a Horn & Hardart restaurant leased the 42nd Street ground floor corner, directly adjoining Rudley's. The competition proved too much for the older restaurant and it closed. Its management asked to be released from the remainder of its lease obligations, which Mr. Durst granted without asking for the customary penalty payment. The little nineteenth-century building still stands, with Rudley's having lost both its restaurant and an opportunity to make a handsome profit.

The address of Durst's building was originally 200 East 42nd Street. When its changed occupancy prompted a name change to the TAMS Building (for a large engineering firm that rented a significant portion of the available space) the address was also changed—to 655 Third Avenue (Figure 77).

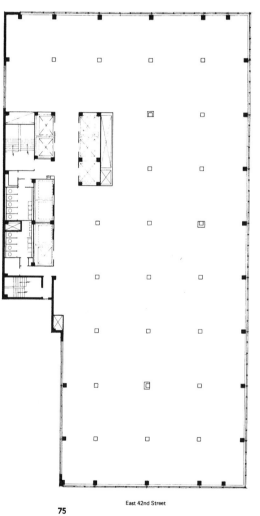

75

74 The site of 200 East 42nd Street before the demolition of the Third Avenue elevated train structure. *(Charles Phelps Cushing, courtesy of The Durst Organization)*

75 A typical floor plan of 655 Third Avenue/200 East 42nd Street showing the notch in the building necessitated by the refusal of Rudley's restaurant to accept a reasonable price to vacate its quarters.

76 The 42nd Street end of what is now the TAMS Building. The five-story holdout building could not become part of the development because of the holdout restaurant on the ground floor. To the left is the Harley Hotel in its final stage of construction. *(Andrew Alpern)*

77 The building at 42nd Street and Third Avenue when it was known as the Lorillard Building. To its left is the small building that held the Rudley's holdout restaurant. *(Photo-File Service, courtesy of The Durst Organization)*

76

77

78

805 Third Avenue

The sleek, ultra-modern office tower—805 Third Avenue—stands in a dramatic contrast to the adjoining two-story restaurant building. The stylized period-architectural feeling of the smaller structure emphasizes its difference in size from its neighbor, and accentuates its position as a holdout (Figure 78). The story began twenty years ago.

In the early 1960s, Seymour Durst began an assemblage of the easterly blockfront of Third Avenue from 49th Street to 50th Street. Following a mode of operation that he had found successful on earlier projects, Mr. Durst hoped to acquire sufficient plottage for a major office building during a soft period for real estate prices, with the intention of holding the property until a propitious time for developing it with a new structure. He was able to buy practically all of the site he had in mind, but was unwilling to pay the price demanded for the corner building occupied by Manny Wolf's restaurant. Wolf's was a very successful operation so there was no pressure to sell the property unless a price could be received that would be an adequate recompense for the loss of the business.

There were two other restaurants on the block including the prestigious Lafayette, an haute cuisine French eatery which maintained a rigid dress code for its patrons. Although Mr. Durst had bought the buildings in which the two restaurants were located, their owners were unwilling to part with their leases. Accordingly, plans were drawn for demolishing the upper floors of the building and bridging over them with steel girders.

Before Mr. Durst's plans for the site went much beyond the preliminary planning stages, developer Arthur Collins contracted to buy the property Mr. Durst had assembled. At the same time—mid-1972—Mr. Collins negotiated successfully with the proprietor of Manny Wolf's to buy the corner restaurant site as well. A plan for an office building on the entire blockfront was developed (Figure 79), but Mr. Collins was unable to complete his financing in time to prevent the two contracts from lapsing.

With the office building project no longer imminent, and with a slowing in the real estate market, Mr. Durst replaced the parking lot he had already constructed on the site with a one-story "taxpayer" store structure. He felt that a new office building would be inappropriate for at least five years, so he wrote store leases for that period. During that time, the Manny Wolf's restaurant property was sold to the people who established Smith & Wollensky.

Smith & Wollensky Following the expiration of the store leases, the "taxpayer" was razed. The two resident restaurants on the Durst property had also moved out, enabling their buildings to be taken down as well. The entire property—minus the Smith & Wollensky building of course—was then leased to Cohen Brothers Realty. The terms of the lease permitted Sherman and Edward Cohen to erect either an office building or a residential one. The Cohens bought the extra unused development rights from the adjoining Amster Yard complex—a group of low buildings—and then decided to erect an office building. To augment the allowable building bulk, the Cohen brothers negotiated with the city to obtain a zoning variance, using the services of John Zuchotti. Mr. Zuchotti was a lawyer who had been head of the City Planning Commission and was skilled in matters of zoning.

Since Smith & Wollensky had a vested interest in the outcome of the proceedings, they hired another former Planning Commission chairman—Donald Elliott—to represent them. While continuing their discussions with the city, the Cohens expanded their potential development package by purchasing Smith & Wollensky's unbuilt rights, paying almost $2 million for them.

Before the negotiations had been completed with the city, an office building was planned and leases were signed. The building design contemplated the maximum possible structure on the site, but the city's ultimate decision was to permit four stories fewer than had already been rented out. Cohen Brothers was forced to renegotiate its leases, but the project proceeded nonetheless, and ultimately the Cohens completed their ownership package by purchasing the fee interest in the land from The Durst Organization.

79

78 The sleek new office structure at 805 Third Avenue during its construction stands in stark contrast to the adjacent restaurant holdout building of Smith & Wollensky. *(Andrew Alpern)*

79 An architectural rendering of the full-block structure planned by Laird Properties in 1972 at 801 Third Avenue. This predecessor to 805 Third Avenue was a scheme that encompassed the corner restaurant site then occupied by Manny Wolf's Steak House. It was never built because suitable financing could not be obtained. *(Emery Roth & Sons, architect)*

80

Sperry-Rand Building

Knapp real estate development firm decided to take advantage of the incipient expansion of the Rockefeller Center complex by erecting a hotel on the easterly block of Sixth Avenue from 51st Street to 52nd Street. Planning on naming the hotel after himself, Mr. Zeckendorf together with his agents began to buy the properties comprising the intended site . . . at ever-increasing prices as news of the project leaked out.

Toots Shor Toots Shor was a flamboyant restaurateur whose well-known establishment occupied its own building on a 40-foot-wide plot at 51

81

80 The north side of 51st Street near Sixth Avenue on March 7, 1939. A large sign reading "Plot for Rent" affixed to numbers 51 and 53 offers "Attractive Terms, Long Lease or Will Sell," and gives the telephone number of the owner, Charles F. Noyes. *(Courtesy of The New-York Historical Society)*

81 The same site on December 14, 1940, showing the new restaurant Toots Shor erected on the plot he had rented from Mr. Noyes. A comment on the times is reflected in the nearby restaurant sign of "The Schooner" that is still offering lunch for 50¢ and dinner for 75¢. *(Courtesy of The New-York Historical Society)*

82 1290 Sixth Avenue and the Toots Shor holdout.

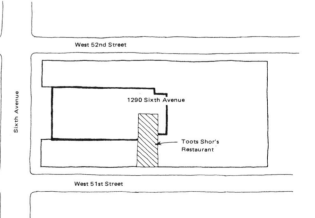

82

West 51st Street. Mr. Shor had taken a net lease on the land from its owner Charles F. Noyes in 1939 and had demolished the two brownstones there to make room for his new restaurant structure (Figures 80 and 81). When Mr. Zeckendorf first approached him nine years remained on his lease, putting Mr. Shor in a very strong position. The developer realized this so he offered $500,000 for the lease. Mr. Shor was in the middle of the block and was convinced he held a key plot (Figure 82). He reasoned that no builder would want to try to build around him, as could be done more conveniently with a holdout on a corner of a building site. Moreover, he had a vigorous restaurant business with a faithful following so he was in no hurry.

Mr. Zeckendorf kept negotiating, continually raising his offer. In the meantime, he worked on Mr. Noyes to obtain ownership of the fee interest. Not a man to go to excessive extremes, Mr. Noyes parted with his interest for $1 million. Even with the deed, however, Mr. Zeckendorf still couldn't demolish the building, so he resumed negotiating with the restaurant owner. It took almost a year, but finally Toots Shor agreed to move . . . for a cash payment of $1.5 million. Mr. Zeckendorf finally got his holdout building, but for a total price of $625 per square foot of land.

In a complete anticlimax, the combination of the delays and the huge outlays of cash necessary to assemble the site put Mr. Zeckendorf into such a bind that he was forced to abandon the hotel project.

Rockefeller Center Inc. then acquired the partially excavated site in a joint venture arrangement with the Uris Building Corporation. Although the high cost of the property could not support a hotel as had been originally planned, it was acceptable for an office project. Fortuitously, the Sperry-Rand Corporation needed a large amount of office space at that point. The result was 1290 Sixth Avenue, named the Sperry-Rand Building for its prime tenant, and initially part of the Rockefeller Center complex (Figure 83). Later, the Uris Corporation bought out its partner Rockefeller Center Inc., and the building lost the distinction of using the special Center postal zipcode. Subsequently, the building was purchased by the Canadian-based, family-owned development firm of Olympia & York. The Reichman brothers who bought 1290 Sixth Avenue probably didn't realize that the building might not have existed, with a hotel there in its stead, if Toots Shor hadn't held out so long and demanded such a high price (Figure 84).

83

83 The office building at 1290 Sixth Avenue whose site encompasses the lot on which the holdout Toots Shor restaurant once stood. *(Jeff Kellner, courtesy of Olympia & York properties)*

84 Bronze plaque at the 51st Street entrance to 1290 Sixth Avenue commemorating the original site of Toots Shor's restaurant. *(Andrew Alpern)*

84

747 Third Avenue

On the face, a commercial holdout might be expected to be reluctant to sell solely because of questions of money. For Rose Resteghini, the question was not money but survival—her own survival.

Mrs. Resteghini emigrated from Parma, Italy, in 1908. She met her husband Joe when both were working in the kitchens of the old Astor Hotel on Times Square. Then in 1914 they opened their first restaurant on 45th Street near Third Avenue. It was no more than a modest eating space behind the grocery store they ran, but it thrived until the building it was in was torn down. They moved to a new location around the corner on Third Avenue, but later had to move again because of the landlord's demolition plans. Finally, they moved to 745 Third Avenue, between 46th Street and 47th Street, eventually buying the entire five-story building (Figure 85).

Joe & Rose Restaurant Rose Resteghini made the restaurant her entire life right from the start, always being part of the planning, cooking, and operation of the place. Her son Freddie grew up among the pots and pans, and after Joe Resteghini died, Freddie and his wife Rena joined Rose as a full-time restaurant operating team. Except for their regular three-week vacations in August each year, they faithfully served good food at reasonable prices to a loyal clientele.

In 1969, William Kaufman and his two sons completed the acquisition of the easterly Third Avenue blockfront between 46th Street and 47th Street with the intention of erecting a new office building on the site. Completed, that is, except for the Resteghinis' building (Figure 86). Negotiations between the 75-year-old Mr. Kaufman and the 80-year-old Mrs. Resteghini were amicable, but Mrs. Resteghini made it quite clear that any deal which would take her out of her kitchen would be rejected.

Mr. Kaufman, himself equally devoted to his real estate business, was un-

85

87

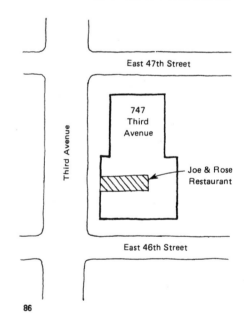

86

85 Joe & Rose Restaurant at 745 Third Avenue before William Kaufman engulfed their quarters with his new office building known as 747 Third Avenue. *(Courtesy of Rose Resteghini)*

86 747 Third Avenue and the Joe & Rose Restaurant.

87 The tenacious restaurant of Rose Resteghini after all the surrounding buildings had been demolished. *(Courtesy of Rose Resteghini)*

derstanding. "This wasn't a routine real estate holdout," said Mr. Kaufman.

We were dealing with emotions, not logic, so we acted accordingly. We did try to convince Rose that it would be best for all concerned to tear down her restaurant and then give her a lease for a new, modern place in our building. But that would have meant that she would have been out of business for more than a year. During that time, Rose wouldn't have lost any money—she's a rich woman anyhow—but that really didn't mean anything to her. She just didn't want to stay out of her kitchen that long, and I respected her feelings.

For her part, Mrs. Resteghini was adament. "This place is my life," she stated flatly.

Every beam and table holds a memory for me. I was offered a lot of money to pack up my pots and leave, but I just couldn't do it. Twice before I had to move and go into business somewhere else, because buildings were coming down. This time, I decided I wasn't going anywhere for anybody.

Under the terms of the arrangement developed to meet the requirements of both the builder and the restaurateur, the upper floors of the Resteghinis' building were removed, and the foundation strengthened and protected (Figure 87). The office building was built to surround completely the remaining ground floor, and the restaurant remained open during the entire construction period, despite some frightening moments during the blasting phase (Figure 88). The Resteghinis received a cash payment plus a twenty-year lease on the restaurant—with an option to renew. Rose Resteghini then continued to rule the kitchen and see that the traditions she began in 1914 were continued (Figure 89).

88

88 During the construction of 747 Third Avenue, the Joe & Rose Restaurant continued to operate. *(Madison Avenue magazine)*

89 The completed office structure at 747 Third Avenue with the venerable Italian restaurant of the Resteghini family still in residence and continuing its uninterrupted operation. *(Andrew Alpern)*

89

520 Madison Avenue

A viable business whose success is perceived by its owner as being closely tied to its location is a formidable obstacle to the assemblage of sufficient land for a substantial development project. And when the business is a family-operated restaurant, thirty-four years at the same location, whose management chores have been willingly assumed by the 38-year-old son of the founder, it takes persistence and a great deal of money out of the pocket of the developer for a deal to be structured.

The Reidys' Restaurant Maurice Reidy opened the Reidys' Restaurant in 1947 as an inexpensive American-Irish bar and eatery with a friendly atmosphere. He worked hard and built up a good business. His son William grew up in and around the family restaurant, so it was logical that he should continue the successful operation begun by his father.

The Reidys' building at 22 East 54th Street began in 1875 as a four-story brownstone residence with a basement and a cellar. Later in the century it was sold to a Dr. Jewett who lived there until the very early 1900s. Recognizing the increasing commercialism of the formerly residential neighborhood, Jewett converted the building to commercial use just before the start of World War I. He extended the front of the building several feet and added a new façade incorporating a pair of massive two-story columns supporting a stone entablature that spanned the width of the building. On that stone he placed bronze letters reading *JEWETT BUILDING*. The floor levels were altered to be more compatible with the new use of the structure, yielding five full floors plus the cellar (Figure 90). Later, an elevator was installed, and at that time a sixth floor was added in the form of a penthouse.

Maurice Reidy's landlord for the first two years of his restaurant's existence was the estate of Dr. Jewett. He had two more landlords until 1966, when he and the Phelps-Stokes Fund jointly bought the building in the form of a commercial condominium.

In 1972, Robert Tishman and Jerry Speyer began to acquire property around the Reidys', hoping to assemble the entire westerly blockfront of Madison Avenue from 53rd Street to 54th Street for an office tower (Figure 91). By 1975, all but the Reidys' building and the corner structure at 54th Street had been bought, but the market was no longer suitable for a speculative building venture so a parking lot was created and the developers waited (Figure 92). Meanwhile, Manny Duell, a speculative real estate investor in his own right, acquired

92

90 A publicity photograph of 22 East 54th Street after its early-twentieth-century conversion to the Jewett Building. *(Courtesy of Brown Harris Stevens)*

91 The design model of 520 Madison Avenue. *(Louis Cheokman, courtesy of Swanke Hayden Connell & Partners)*

92 A view of 22 East 54th Street before the construction of 520 Madison Avenue forced removal of its upper floors. The original line of the front of the building can be discerned in the brickwork exposed at the side of the structure. *(Andrew Alpern)*

an option on the corner building and attempted to create a holdout situation against the Tishman/Speyer group. This maneuver failed, the building changed hands, and in February 1979 Tishman and Speyer bought it. Then the negotiations shifted to the building the Reidys occupied, as the last remaining holdout (Figure 93).

The Phelps-Stokes Fund readily sold its condominium share in the building, impressively increasing its endowment in the process. Realizing that they were in a particularly advantageous position, Maurice Reidy and his son William sought to maximize what they might be able to extract from the deal by hiring an architectural consultant to assist with the background research for their negotiations. The architect studied the site and the zoning regulations to determine how the acquisition of the Reidys' development rights would affect the possible size of the new office building. With this information and many financial assumptions, the Reidys decided just how valuable they thought their building might be to the developers. Considering their figures to be good ammunition, the father and son sat down to negotiate with the Tishman/Speyer interests. The arrangement that emerged from the negotiations was unusually complex and expensive, but it gave the developers a building which they hoped would be able to justify their investment, while enabling the Reidys' Restaurant to continue operation at the same site and to expand as well.

Since the Reidys did not consider that any alternative location would be equivalent to the one they already had, the restauranteurs and the developers sought a solution at the new office tower's site. A brand new building for the restaurant at the corner of the site was considered, since it wouldn't interfere with the office structure, but the cost of such a plan proved prohibitive.

The final agreement gave to the Reidys the ability to remain in their existing quarters and to continue operation during the construction of the office building. It also gave to them an additional 4000 square feet of space, extending the usable area of their cellar and their two dining floors into the new structure. A new private elevator serving the restaurant and new stairways for the Reidys were constructed within the new building, enabling these elements in the original building to be removed, yielding more effective space for the dining rooms. Access was also provided to the building's truck loading dock, ending the thirty-year necessity of wheeling deliveries through the restaurant. The family retains ownership of the space in the

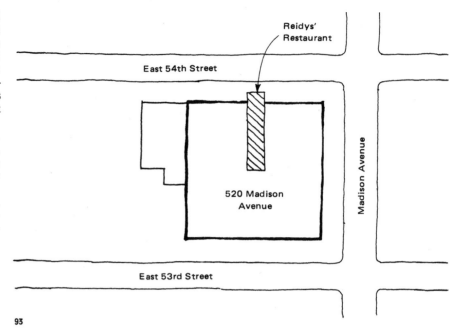

93

93 The Reidys' Restaurant and 520 Madison Avenue.

94 (a) & (b) The original plans of the first and second floors of 22 East 54th Street after the building had been remodeled for commercial use. *(Courtesy of Brown Harris Stevens)*

95 (a) & (b) The first and second floors of the Reidys' Restaurant showing the additional space gained within the new structure of 520 Madison Avenue. *(Courtesy of Swanke Hayden Connell & Partners)*

old building, and has a ninety-nine-year lease on the added space in the new structure (Figures 94 and 95).

The developers obtained the right to remove the upper portion of the building just above Dr. Jewett's stone entablature, and to use the excess development rights for additional footage on the Reidys' lot beyond what the restaurant already occupied. Since these things had been of no practical use to Maurice and William Reidy anyway, all they really gave up was some of their peace and quiet during the construction of the office building (Figure 96).

In an effort to attract the patronage of the new building's construction workers and to counter any rumors that they

might be giving way to the new structure, the Reidys were active with a small public relations program. It started with signs on the sides of their building announcing that they weren't moving, and included a humorous "explanation" of why the old building's upper floors were being removed (Figures 97 and 98).

To the casual passer-by, the office building developed by Tishman/Speyer looks quite normal (and in fact it is) except for a small two-story appendage jutting out ten feet from the north facade—a relic more than a century old that represents either a living advertisement for the Reidys' Restaurant or an aesthetic eyesore, depending on one's point of view (Figure 99).

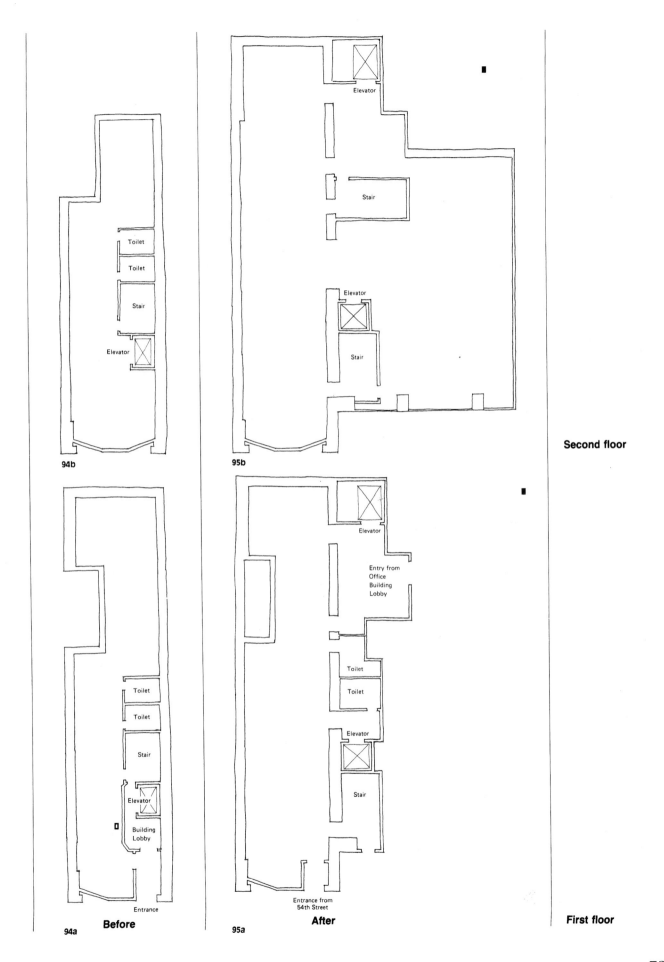

Toilet

Toilet

Stair

Elevator

94b

Elevator

Stair

Elevator

Stair

95b

Toilet

Toilet

Stair

Elevator

Building
Lobby

Entrance

94a   **Before**

Elevator

Entry from
Office
Building
Lobby

Toilet

Toilet

Elevator

Stair

Entrance from
54th Street

95a   **After**

Second floor

First floor

96

97

96 The building at 520 Madison Avenue under construction, showing the necessity of special structural provisions in the building's steel framework to accommodate the holdout. *(Andrew Alpern)*

97 This sign appeared on the side of the building housing the Reidys' Restaurant shortly after construction plans for 520 Madison Avenue were announced. *(Andrew Alpern)*

98 A sign devised by Maurice and William Reidy to "explain" why the upper portion of their building was being removed. *(Andrew Alpern)*

99 The Reidys' Restaurant surviving as a holdout against 520 Madison Avenue. *(Gil Amiaga)*

98

26 Broadway

In 1796, the town residence of Alexander Hamilton stood on the site of 26 Broadway. Fifty years later a coal yard occupied the land, but in 1886, John Davison Rockefeller erected his Standard Oil Building there, to the designs of architect Ebenezer L. Roberts. Its nine stories were adequate until the company's growth necessitated an increase in the building's height to fifteen stories in 1896, along with an expansion of the structure to the north. For this project, Mr. Rockefeller used the services of the architectural firm of Kimball & Thompson (Figure 100).

The significant growth of the Standard Oil Company over the next twenty-five years dictated a major expansion of the building. Early in the 1920s, the firms of Carrère & Hastings and Shreve, Lamb & Blake were retained to design a new building that would incorporate the old one. Since the oil company had acquired all of the needed land in fee or by lease, the designers assumed they had free rein to plan whatever sort of building they felt would be appropriate (Figure 101).

Childs Restaurant After preliminary designs were presented, however, it was found that a tenant in one of the buildings scheduled for demolition had declined to move out. A Childs Restaurant occupied the ground floor at 3 Beaver Street and enjoyed a prosperous business (Figure 102). Since Childs held a valid lease with several years left to run, the restaurant's management decided it would be more advantageous to remain than to accept the relocation price offered by the Rockefeller interests.

Rather than postpone construction of the new building, the architects redesigned it in a form that permitted the Childs building to remain. Construction of the huge new Standard Oil Building was finished in 1925, except for the section on its south side that surrounded the Beaver Street holdout (Figure 103). The architects had replanned 26 Broadway to form a cavelike opening from which protruded the anachronistic five-story building that housed the restaurant (Figures 104 and 105).

The Childs lease expired in 1928, and shortly thereafter the old building was razed. Then 26 Broadway was finally completed according to the plans drawn several years earlier (Figure 106).

100 The fifteen-story building of the Standard Oil Company prior to its expansion in 1925 to form the 26 Broadway that now exists. *(Collection of Andrew Alpern)*

101 A rendering of the version of 26 Broadway designed in 1921 under the assumption that there would be no holdouts on the site. This scheme presented a solid façade along Beaver Street giving the building a more substantial appearance than was possible when the Childs Restaurant refused to move. *(Collection of Andrew Alpern)*

102 Broadway and Beaver Street, c. 1923. The original section of 26 Broadway is at the extreme left. The Childs Restaurant holdout is behind the white-framed show window in the five-story building at 3 Beaver Street. Bowling Green is in the foreground. *(Irving Underhill, courtesy of Bevin Koeppel)*

103 A 1925 view of the newly finished extension to 26 Broadway with the little Beaver Street holdout still in existence. The earlier section of the giant building retained its original dark 1890s façade in this photograph. The facing and windows were later replaced to conform to the classical limestone design of the rest of the structure. *(Wurts, courtesy of the Museum of the City of New York)*

104 The holdout building at 3 Beaver Street surrounded by a "cave" formed by the walls of the truncated 26 Broadway. *(The Sun Printing and Publishing Association)*

100

101

103

102

104

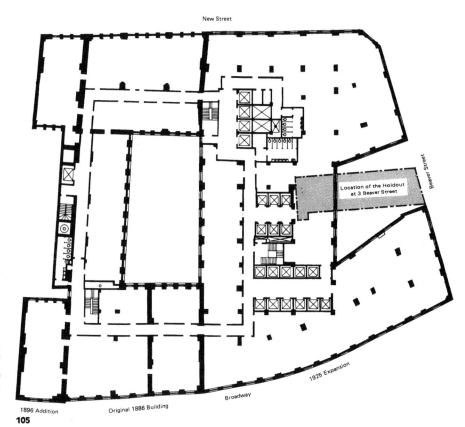

105 A typical full-floor plan of 26 Broadway indicating the 1886 original building, the 1896 addition, and the 1925 expansion. The position of the holdout determined the location of the courtyard, while the rear portion affected the placement of the elevators and the structural columns. *(Courtesy of Donald Weill)*

105

New Street

Location of the Holdout at 3 Beaver Street

Beaver Street

1925 Expansion

Broadway

1896 Addition

Original 1886 Building

106 The completed 26 Broadway following the removal of Childs Restaurant and the 3 Beaver Street holdout building. Beaver Street is at the right in the picture; the position of the open court on that side of the building was determined by the location of the holdout. *(Morris Rosenfeld, courtesy of Bevin Koeppel)*

106

450 Seventh Avenue

107 The Nelson Tower at 450 Seventh Avenue planned for developer Julius Nelson as a full-block structure by architect H. Craig Severance. Completed in 1931, the reality of the finished building did not match the conception because of the corner holdout. *(Andrew Alpern)*

107

Cobble Court

The fate of most holdout buildings is either to stand firm in the face of opposition and prevent or inhibit development, or to give way to progress and be destroyed in the process. One tiny holdout on the Upper East Side succumbed to the need of its site for other purposes, but it did not die. Instead, it merely moved to a new location in the West Village.

This peripatetic structure is said to be a survivor from the eighteenth century—possibly a farmhouse—but no firm evidence of this has been uncovered. Its definite history is known only to date from the 1860s when it was bought by William and Margaret Glass. This couple moved from Greenwich Village to what was then a very rural part of the city, occupying the little frame dwelling set well back from the intersection of 71st Street and York Avenue (then known as Avenue A). Mr. and Mrs. Glass operated a dairy which brought them enough success to permit them to build a larger and more substantial house at 1335 York Avenue. This new home was directly in front of the old one, hiding it from the view of passers-by. The Glasses lived in the front house and rented out the one in back.

The Glass children were born and raised in 1335 York Avenue, as were the grandchildren. One of those, Mrs. Margaret Glass Healy, inherited 1335 together with the wooden house in the backyard. The older building continued to be rented out—for a time as a restaurant, known as Cobble Court for the old cobblestones that paved the area around the little structure.

In 1960, Sven Bernhard rented the little house for $65 per month. It had deteriorated over the years—both structurally and cosmetically—and Mr. Bernhard and his wife Ingrid, owners of a travel agency, set about restoring it for themselves. Three years of work resulted in a charmingly livable cottage of six rooms.

During this time, Mrs. Healy was being courted for her property by the Archbishopric of New York. Since 1952, the Catholic group had been attempting to purchase the entire York Avenue block-front from 71st to 72nd Streets for a new Mary Manning Walsh Home for the Aged to replace the home's obsolescent building at 420 East 59th Street. Most of the assemblage had been completed, but Margaret Glass Healy was reluctant to sell the two buildings that had been in her family for more than a century. Finally in 1967, Mrs. Healy yielded, and accepted $75,000 for the 25-foot by 75-foot piece of land with its two houses.

Distressed at the prospect of losing the cozy cottage on which they had labored so long and hard, Sven and Ingrid Bernhard held on. They brought to a halt the demolition going on around them because they refused to accept the $600 relocation fee proffered by John J. Reynolds Inc., the real estate brokers hired by the Archbishopric to clear the site. The Bernhards recognized that their position was ultimately untenable, however, so they searched for some solution. The answer lay in their purchase of an awkward 3600-square-foot triangular plot of land at the corner of Charles Street and Greenwich Street in the West Village. Six small four- and five-story houses had formerly stood there, but the Bernhards were able to acquire the site completely vacant. They then obtained from the Archbishopric the right to remove the little old house from its York Avenue location, along with the cobblestones that surrounded it. Finally, at a cost of $6500, the venerable structure was trussed up, put onto a low-slung flatbed trailer, and trucked along a five-mile route to its new home, now a bucolic suburban setting of grass, trees, and flowering vines (Figure 108). William and Margaret Glass left this same section of Greenwich Village to live in the little frame house; had they been willing to wait 110 years, the house would have come to them.

108 The diminutive frame house of uncertain age that Sven Bernhard restored and then moved from York Avenue and 71st Street to its present location at 121 Charles Street at the corner of Greenwich Street in the West Village. (*Andrew Alpern*)

Bank of America Building

For years, the venerable Biltmore Hotel on Madison Avenue near Grand Central Terminal played an important part in New York's social life. It was a proper and convenient place to stay, and was a center for balls, parties, and private rendezvous. But in the search by real estate investors for the "highest and best use" of a piece of property, tradition and sentiment must take a back seat to economics. When the Milstein family took ownership of the building in 1980, hotel rooms were not as profitable as office space. Ergo, conversion.

In 1982, the building was stripped to its steel frame for reconstruction as a headquarters building for the Bank of America. All, that is, except for a tiny two-room bookshop tucked away on the 43rd Street side of the building (Figure 109). By one means or another, all the other occupants of the hotel had been ousted before the demolition work had begun, but the diminutive store successfully resisted all removal efforts. Run by two serene nuns of the order of the Daughters of St. Paul, the St. Paul's Catholic Book and Film Center braved the turmoil of construction all around and remained rooted to the spot throughout the period of rebuilding. A sign was placed on the door reading "Thanks to your prayers we will remain in this location during the period of renovation. God bless you." (Figure 110). Whether it was prayer or hard bargaining that won the day is debatable, but for the little religious holdout the question is irrelevant. The bookstore remains, and that is all the nuns care about.

St. Paul's Book and Film Center

109

109 The former Biltmore Hotel in the midst of its metamorphosis into the Bank of America building at 335 Madison Avenue. During a lunchtime work break on the sunny 43rd Street side of the site, the construction appurtenances almost totally obscure the little holdout store. *(Andrew Alpern)*

110 The entrance to the religious bookshop that refused to leave its quarters in the Biltmore Hotel during the reconstruction process is hard to find behind the contractor's barricades. *(Andrew Alpern)*

110

16 East 46th Street

H. P. Kraus was a rare-book dealer in prewar Vienna. When the Nazis took over that city in 1938, Kraus was betrayed by one of his employees and was sent to concentration camps for a year and a half. Unable to recover his stock or his quarters following his release, he went first to Sweden and then to the United States, where his wartime experiences with insecurity and impermanence virtually guaranteed his eventual status as a determined holdout.

After having orchestrated a coup in obtaining several libraries of czarist Russian books and selling them at a significant profit, Mr. Kraus bought a formerly residential brownstone at 16 East 46th Street and converted it for use as a showroom for his rare book business with his offices and storerooms on the upper floors. Seeking to reestablish the ambience of his Austrian shop of the early 1930s, he furnished both the public and the private rooms of his new shop with oriental rugs, antique furniture and decorative accessories, and elegant wood paneling and bookcases. Under these conditions it was not surprising that he refused to sell his property to a developer who wanted to expand his office-building site lying to the east of Mr. Kraus's nineteenth-century structure (Figure 111).

Later, he parried a threatened assemblage to the west of his building by buying the eight-story building situated directly adjacent to his own business home. Imperious to the point of arrogance, Mr. Kraus sees nothing strange in his insistence on retaining his book business in a very unbookish environment among high-rise office structures. His book dealings have brought him considerable wealth and an admirable reputation for both shrewdness and scholarship. The incongruity of his five-story shop building on East 46th Street has brought him publicity and acerbic comments about his eccentricity. Perhaps both aspects of Mr. Kraus are equally important to this man whose position as a holdout seems almost logical in view of his personality and personal history.

111 The anachronistic holdout at 16 East 46th Street. Purchased by Hans Peter Kraus in 1946 and home to his preeminent rare-book business, the structure was originally a high-stooped one-family house. *(Andrew Alpern)*

One Lincoln Plaza

During the mid-1960s a proposal was made to build a landscaped *grande allée* between 63rd Street and 64th Street to connect Lincoln Center for the Performing Arts with Central Park. It was one of those majestic gestures planners sometimes like to make, but was doomed to failure since it would have necessitated demolishing the headquarters building of the venerable Society for Ethical Culture, the school run by the society, and an important and much-used YMCA.

In the aftermath of that ill-fated project, the New York City Planning Commission developed the concept of a special Lincoln Center zoning district. At the same time Seymour Milstein and his family decided to construct a mixed-use office building and apartment tower at the westerly end of what might have become Lincoln Center's ceremonial mall.

Concerned about the "quality of the architectural environment," the Planning Commission made numerous demands on the Milsteins, and dictated what it wanted the size and shape of the new building to be. Rather than prolong the approval process—a costly matter—the Milsteins accepted the design constraints imposed by the Commission, in exchange for assurance of permission to build extra floors on the apartment tower.

Part of the agreement with the city planners required that the Milsteins incorporate a small public park into the building's site development. Not satisfied with that, the commission then demanded that the site on the opposite side of 63rd Street also be purchased and developed with a complementary building so as to double the size of the park. This too the Milsteins agreed to, and they bought the additional land for $7 million. Then they began the foundations for the forty-three-story building they had wanted in the first place. Before the basement work was complete, however, the city attempted to downgrade the zoning and reduce the number of permissable floors. Having reached the end of their tether, the Milsteins took their dispute to the courts, and won. The city prevailed with its zoning changes for the southerly block, however, so the builders refrained from developing it.

33 West 63rd Street While the contretemps with the city officials was developing, the Milsteins were having other problems acquiring the entire site needed for the building. One Colonel Elyachar, an elderly man with extensive real estate holdings throughout New York, owned a five-story tenement house at 33 West 63rd Street and was reluctant to sell. Although the property yielded only $3000 profit a year—which would indicate a fair selling price of no more than $50,000—the Colonel insisted on getting $200,000 for it. The Milsteins agreed to this price, and came to the title closing prepared to pay it. Before the paperwork was finalized, however, Col. Elyachar had upped his demand to $300,000. Suspecting that the price might be raised again, the Milsteins arrived at the next closing session with a check for $400,000. When Col. Elyachar refused even that price, the developers proffered a blank check made out to the Technicon, an Israeli institute of higher learning and Col. Elyachar's favorite charity. They invited him to fill in any amount to be given to the school in his name, but he turned them down. His argument was that because of the capital

gains tax that would have to be paid, the selling price was now too high for him to afford to sell, so he proposed a tax-free exchange for some other building—and he knew just the building he wanted.

On investigation, the building was found to be already under contract to another buyer. The deal could be broken, but it would be costly. After much negotiation, the deed was obtained, at a cost of $600,000. The Milsteins brought the deed to the fifth title closing, prepared at last to transfer it to Col. Elyachar in exchange for his $3000-a-year tenement. In a final stipulation, however, the colonel demanded a sale-lease-back arrangement that would guarantee him a lifetime income of $50,000 a year. At this point the Milsteins lost patience, told the holdout owner in colorful lan-

guage how absurd his proposal was, and vowed to build without the tenement site (Figure 112).

An interview ten years later yielded much vituperation from Col. Elyachar aimed squarely at the Milsteins, along with rambling stories of the affair. After several sessions, Col. Elyachar settled on a version in which he insisted that he

112 The building at 33 West 63rd Street, with naked sides that were never intended to be exposed. Stripped of its original cornice, alone and forlorn, it is a sad holdout attempting to hide its shabbiness with a pathetic wooden fence. *(Andrew Alpern)*

never had any intention of selling. "I never sell anything," he said. "I still own every piece of real estate I ever bought." When asked why he had not been more cooperative with the Milstein family, he claimed he had had a verbal agreement with them to develop the entire property jointly, but that they had backed out without consulting him. Since he felt he had been wronged, he refused to cooperate.

The result of the holdout's intrusion on the site is a peculiar boomerang-shaped building which looms over the little tenement (Figure 113). The forty-three-story tower comes to a point at the southwest corner of the site, but this potentially spectacular architectural feature on each floor is given over to a windowless bathroom—an outgrowth of the contorted planning necessitated by Col. Elyachar's unrealistic demands (Figure 114). What would have been a pleasant public park is now just some bushes attempting to hide the blank side walls of the tenement, and its uncooperative owner is left with his meager cash flow and a lost opportunity.

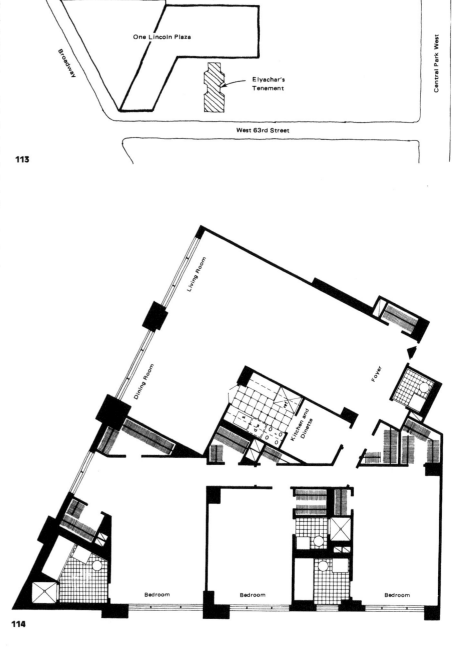

113 The holdout tenement at 33 West 63rd Street blocks what would have been a modest park in front of One Lincoln Plaza.

114 The contorted planning necessitated by the holdout yielded this layout for the corner apartment on each floor of the new tower building. The windowless bathroom hides a potentially spectacular view.

1166 Sixth Avenue

In 1974, the forty-four stories of the office building at 1166 Sixth Avenue were completed. Ordinarily that would signal the beginning of a series of corporate relocations that would fill the building with tenants, but for 1166 that didn't happen. No one moved in for five years, and during that time more than $100 million was lost by some very large companies that had interests in the building (Figure 115). Precisely why this happened is not absolutely clear, but basically the poor state of New York City's business climate at the time 1166 Sixth Avenue was ready for tenants was at the heart of the matter. Perhaps things would have been different if the building had been completed a year earlier, and perhaps that might have happened if Bernard Pravda hadn't spent two years running the builder around in circles, finally forcing him to redesign the project. Perhaps those $100 million wouldn't have been lost if Mr. Pravda hadn't been a recalcitrant holdout. Who can say?

In 1967, Tishman Realty & Construction Corporation joined with Edwin Glickman, who represented a group of investors, to assemble the plot on the easterly side of Sixth Avenue between 45th Street and 46th Street as the site for a speculative office building. One by one the individual parcels were purchased, and where necessary the leases of tenants were also bought. One owner wasn't so easy to buy out, however.

56 West 46th Street Bernard Pravda owned 56 West 46th Street with his brother Alfred, having bought the small five-story loft building in 1963 for $140,000. Henry J. Kassis, a broker representing the Tishman interests, approached Mr. Pravda in August 1967 and offered to buy the building, not mentioning that it was for Mr. Tishman. A price of $170,000 was agreed upon, but later Mr. Pravda reneged, claiming that a restaurant tenant wanted to rent the ground floor. By November the restaurant was installed and the price was increased to $225,000, ostensibly to

115 An architectural rendering of the plain black box designed by Skidmore, Owings & Merrill as 1166 Sixth Avenue. Set back only slightly from the avenue, its obligatory plaza was placed behind the building to accommodate the holdout structure on the side street. After its completion 1166 remained completely vacant for five years—a victim of an inopportune downturn in the real estate market, perhaps exacerbated by the delays caused by the fruitless negotiations with the holdout's owner. *(Skidmore Owings & Merrill)*

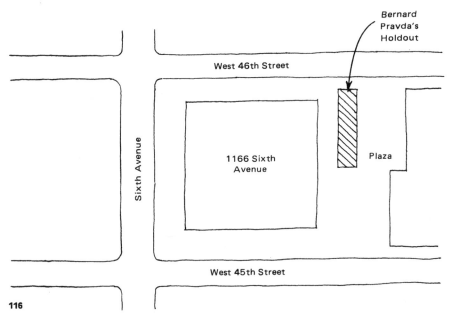

Bernard Pravda's Holdout

Sixth Avenue

1166 Sixth Avenue

Plaza

West 45th Street

116

116 Site plan of 1166 Sixth Avenue.

117 Bernard Pravda's holdout building at 56 West 46th Street during excavation operations for the 1166 Sixth Avenue office tower. *(Patrick A. Burns and* The New York Times*)*

compensate for the $50,000 that was said to have been invested in the restaurant renovations.

Obstacles appeared again and again to prevent the sale, and each time the price went up, first to $386,000, then to $400,000, and then to $450,000 plus $125,000 for the restaurant lease. At this point a tax-free building exchange was proposed, which would have given Mr. Pravda a more valuable building without his having to pay the capital gains tax on the profit from the sale of the old one. This was accepted for a time, but then rejected in favor of a straight price of $505,000. But when a contract was presented, Mr. Pravda's demands went up again. This game kept going until more than a year had passed. Then, in late October 1968, the asking price hit $1 million. More tax-free exchanges were proposed, including one that would have given Mr. Pravda two buildings in place of the one he owned, plus $150,000 besides. Still no agreement was reached and by early October 1969 Mr. Pravda wanted $1 million for the building he had bought six years earlier for less than one-fifth that price.

At this point the Glickman interests sold out to Mr. Tishman, leaving the

117

$42 million. The delay in completing the assemblage was becoming increasingly disturbing to Mr. Tishman, so they pressed Mr. Pravda to finalize the deal. Together they sat down with their lawyers in the Tishman office on Halloween, 1969, and negotiated until 5:30 the following morning, finally agreeing to a price of $1.34 million. Mr. Pravda promptly left for a vacation in the Bahamas, but when his lawyers sent the signed contract back to Mr. Tishman, he had crossed out the typewritten price and inked in a figure of $2,066,000.

Giving up on coming to terms with Bernard Pravda, Mr. Tishman instructed its architects, Skidmore Owings & Merrill, to redesign the new structure to exclude the holdout building. To do this, the designers were forced to move the building to the west, bringing it out almost to the building line at Sixth Avenue (Figure 116). The plaza required by the zoning regulations was relegated to the midblock side of the building where it would be in shadow for most of each day. And disfiguring that plaza would be the derelict appearance of the Pravda holdout (Figure 117). This redesign further added to Mr. Tishman's costs and caused additional delays.

By the time construction had at last begun, the economy had started to slide. When the building was finished, the office market had so dried up that $8.50 per square foot was all that could be realized on space for which Mr. Tishman needed $12 just to break even. Then, the only major potential corporate tenant, General Telephone and Electronics, changed its mind about staying in the city and moved to Connecticut, leaving Mr. Tishman with a very white elephant. Citibank, the construction leader who had put $45 million into the project, was as nervous as Mr. Tishman. For two years, $1 million a month was pumped into the project to keep it alive, but then in the spring of 1976, with New York City on the verge of bankruptcy, both Mr. Tishman and Citibank abandoned the building.

This put the property into the hands of the holder of the mortgage on the land, the New York State Employees' Retirement System. Its director of real estate investment, Leon Braun, needed to recoup the system's investment and he turned to real estate broker Edward S. Gordon for a solution. Mr. Gordon brought together the New York Telephone Company and the Teachers' Insurance and Annuity Association, who bought the building as a commercial condominium. While the Telephone Company wanted the space for its own

118 A model of the little park behind 1166 Sixth Avenue. Called International Paper Plaza for one of the prime tenants of the building, this midtown oasis was designed by landscape architect Hideo Sasaki. An important element of the design is the grove of full-sized trees in the foreground. This miniforest was made possible by the Pravda holdout which formerly stood on that spot. When 1166 was built, a deep basement was constructed under the plaza area, avoiding of course the holdout building. After Bernard Pravda's structure was finally acquired and demolished, its site provided the only place where sufficient below-grade depth was available for the root balls of fully matured trees. *(Courtesy of The Space Design Group)*

use, the teachers' group considered its half as an investment and thus needed a tenant. Mr. Gordon arranged for a lease with the International Paper Company. In 1978, Mr. Gordon finally bought Mr. Pravda's holdout for $850,000, enabling it to be demolished and plans drawn for a redesigned park. That park now forms a separate entrance plaza to International Paper's space and leads directly to the American Crafts Museum

(Figure 118).

It was only because of the razing of the holdout that the new park could be created, and it was that park that convinced International Paper to remain in New York City and move to 1166 Sixth Avenue instead of relocating to Atlanta, Georgia. The final fall of Mr. Pravda's holdout saved 1700 jobs for New York, partially offsetting the $100 million 1166's original investors had lost.

1133 Sixth Avenue

A holdout formed an impediment to the development of 1133 Sixth Avenue, *yet it was a different holdout that provided the impetus for the entire project.*

Alfred King was a professional holdout, following the example of his father who had had protracted negotiations over a particular little plot of land during the creation of the Rockefeller Center complex. He would purchase lots he considered critical to large-scale projects and then sell them to developers for inflated prices.

Mr. King had bought a small midblock building between 43rd Street and 44th Street on the west side of Sixth Avenue. During discussions with developer Seymour Durst in 1964, Mr. King suggested that the assemblage of the entire blockfront might be feasible. He indicated that he would of course be willing to sell the property he owned in the middle of the block . . . but for a holdout price of $200 a square foot.

Mr. Durst liked the idea, and commenced the assemblage process, gradually acquiring the rest of the block at prices that averaged about $125 a foot. At that point he went back to Mr. King, who was true to his word and sold the final lot for the $200 price he had originally quoted.

101 West 43rd Street Although he held a deed to each piece of property on the site, Mr. Durst still had to acquire possession of all the buildings. One by one he was able to vacate each building, until he reached the southerly corner. The entire corner building had been leased to one man by the Chase Manhattan Bank acting as trustee for the previous absentee owner. The upper three floors had been subleased for a hotel operation, and individual subleases had been written for store tenants on the lower two floors. The building operator claimed that the bank had extended his lease before Mr. Durst had taken ownership, and he dug in for a long fight. Mr. Durst brought a suit for possession, but the case dragged on, threatening to halt the project.

Rather than sit by and see money wasted on the rest of the site while the lawsuit was settled, Mr. Durst instructed his architect, Emery Roth & Sons, to modify the office building's design to enable the construction to proceed around the holdout. This was accomplished by setting the new building back from the Sixth Avenue building line and planning two symmetrical, one-story flanking pavilions. The northerly one, designed to accommodate the needs of the American Savings Bank which had formerly owned a piece of the site, was built concurrently with the rest of the structure, but the southerly one was constructed later, after possession of the holdout had finally been accomplished.

With the new design approved by the city authorities, foundation excavations began around the holdout on the corner. While this was going on, a small building adjoining the site of a building under construction at 1700 Broadway collapsed into the excavation next to it, with the loss of several lives. The New York City Building Department immediately ordered a halt to the work at 1133 Sixth Avenue, fearing that a similar disaster might occur there.

Confronted with a seemingly hopeless situation, Mr. Durst cast about to find a solution that would permit him to proceed with the excavation for the new building. One engineer after another offered suggestions, but none was willing to stand behind his theory and offer any assurance of success. Finally, one engineer proposed that the old holdout building be reinforced with wooden timbers and then strapped together with steel cables . . . and he was willing to guarantee the safety of his suggestion. The city accepted the concept, it was effected, and construction was permitted to resume (Figures 119 and 120).

Ultimately, the corner building was taken down and the new one completed according to the modified plans (Figure 121). The memory of the holdout persists in the configuration of the office building, but the net result of the lessee's intransigence was the added cost inherent in the necessity to protect the old building and to construct the new one in two separate pieces. The time lost and the delays in completing the project affected the interim carrying costs as well, all of which were translated into higher rents for the tenants who eventually moved into the office tower. All that the holdout operator gained was the excitement of the legal battle, and all the subtenants could show were the missed heartbeats every time the dynamite went off for the excavation blasting.

119

120

121

119 The holdout building at 101 West 43rd Street during the construction of 1133 Sixth Avenue. Clearly visible are the bracing timbers and the cables encircling the building to help hold it together during the blasting and excavation operations. *(Norman R. Harrison, courtesy of The Durst Organization)*

120 The steelwork being erected for 1133 Sixth Avenue with the five-story holdout at the 43rd Street corner of the site. *(Norman R. Harrison, courtesy of The Durst Organization)*

121 The building at 1133 Sixth Avenue as presented by its architect. The position of the building on its site was an outgrowth of the presence of a holdout structure at the 43rd Street corner. *(Hanrahan, courtesy of Seymour Durst)*

875 Third Avenue

In 1968, Edwin Glickman of Madison Associates began the laborious job of assembling the entire block defined by 52nd Street, 53rd Street, Second Avenue, and Third Avenue. Since he knew the process would take several years, his plans for the property were not firm, but one possibility that was discussed was a pair of giant buildings—one at each avenue-end of the block—connected by a public arcade with shops and other amenities. It was anticipated that the building at the Third Avenue end would be an office structure, while the one at Second Avenue would be residential.

Over a period of a few years, about half the block was assembled, but the process of acquiring possession did not go smoothly. Most of the existing buildings were residential, and many of the tenants had lived in their apartments for many years and enjoyed rents artificially depressed by the rent control laws. In an effort to expedite the removal process, Urban Relocation Corporation was hired to vacate the buildings. That company's tactics were strong, and aroused the ire of both residents and civic watchdogs alike. Youthful drug abusers attempting rehabilitation were given the use of partially vacated buildings at little or no rent, and building services were allowed to deteriorate. An article appeared in a popular magazine spotlighting some of the problems, and Urban Relocation was the subject of an investigation by the authorities. By the time the dust had settled, many of the buildings were still occupied, and the market for high-rise office space had softened to a point where the project was no longer viable.

By 1980, economic factors in New York City had recovered, and an office building was again a potentially profitable venture. Madison Associates had become Madison Equities, and Robert Gladstone had replaced Edwin Glickman as the driving force for the project. Mr. Gladstone realigned his firm's holdings on the block and retained the Chicago office of Skidmore Owings & Merrill to serve as architect.

The Third Avenue blockfront was the obvious site for the proposed office building, with a potential direct connection to the subway station at the 53rd Street corner an obvious plus. With ownership of all the needed buildings in the hands of Madison Equities, all appeared to be well-in-hand. But despite significant inducements that were offered, several long-term lessees refused to be bought out. Particularly sensitive to the adverse publicity of a decade earlier, the firm decided to build around the holdouts rather than attempt to apply pressure.

The architect was then confronted with the problem of creating a distinctive building on an awkward site that would take maximum advantage of the zoning regulations and allowances. The building had to work well and be initially attractive, while being capable of appropriate expansion when the last of the leases expires and the holdout buildings are taken down—something that may not happen until 1990.

What Skidmore Owings & Merrill's design partner Bruce Graham created was a multisided building that wraps around the five little corner holdout buildings. Following the example of the earlier multiuse Galleria project of Madison Equities on East 57th Street, Graham designed a large entrance atrium accessible to the public. But then he repeated the same concept of a multistoried open garden space three more times, stacking them at intervals within the building. The result is an unusual building that makes the best of a difficult constraint. And the builder and the public can look forward to the removal of the obtrusive old structures in a few years, and the completion of the architect's original design concept (Figures 122, 123, and 124).

122 Site plan of 875 Third Avenue.

123 A model of the office tower at 875 Third Avenue as first proposed. The stacked atria show clearly at the southwesterly side of the building. As the design later developed, the structure was extended at the left through to 53rd Street, surrounding the four corner holdouts on Third Avenue and the one on the side street. The model's depiction of the older buildings on the avenue is incorrect. *(Gil Amiaga)*

124 The structural steelwork for 875 Third Avenue rising in its unusual shape necessitated by the holdouts at the corner of 53rd Street. *(Andrew Alpern)*

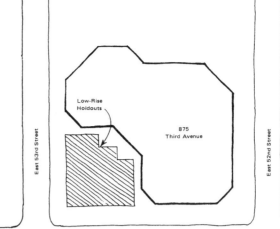

122

123

124

825 Third Avenue

The site plan of the land which was developed at 825 Third Avenue is remarkably similar in shape to what was built upon at 875 Third Avenue two blocks further north. There is an important difference, however. At 875, the encumbered corner parcels were merely temporarily occupied by lessees, while at 825, the corner buildings could not be purchased at all, since earlier attempts by other developers to assemble the site had driven the asking prices out of sight.

The difference in the buildings that were newly constructed is obvious (Figure 125). Not quite so obvious is the difference in the holdouts. The three modest old buildings are at the corner of 51st Street adjoining 825. Following the completion of the office tower, the holdout owners felt that the value of their holdings had climbed almost as high as the new building itself. The resultant series of rent increases to which the stores and upper-floor commercial space was subjected yielded a rapid succession of tenants. Their high-priced but insubstantial nature has not been a benefit to the neighborhood. Sadly, this is often the outcome of a real estate impasse brought about by a holdout (Figure 126).

125 Number 825 Third Avenue is oriented toward 50th Street to avoid the relics at the 51st Street side that could not be bought. *(Kempa, courtesy of Seymour Durst)*

126 The development of 825 Third Avenue was the impetus for a succession of rent increases in the three little holdout buildings at the 51st Street end of the block. The resultant turnover in tenancy of the stores has been a detriment to the neighborhood. *(Andrew Alpern)*

125

126

Broadway at 97th Street

During the latter part of the nineteenth century, real estate development worked its way north on the Upper West Side, preceded by land speculators. Much of the area was open country, checkerboarded by the newly opened streets and dotted with old frame dwellings (Figure 127). As the land was subdivided, sold, and resold, some owners improved their property while others held it vacant, waiting for values to rise.

This was particularly true along Broadway, where the growth of a grand avenue of splendid residences was anticipated; West End Avenue was expected to become the commercial street serving the homes on Broadway. The expected development didn't happen that way, and as the landowners recognized this, they stopped waiting and built what seemed most appropriate at the time.

One block that remained virtually vacant almost until the turn of the twentieth century was the westerly one along Broadway from 97th to 98th Streets. The various lots which comprised the block were transferred several times before there was any building activity. The corner property that fronted 25 feet on 97th Street and 100 feet along Broadway was bought in 1896 by Gustav Stillgebauer with his wife Elizabeth and his sister Henrietta. A short time later they decided that the time was propitious for development, and in 1899 they erected

a two-story commercial structure with seven small stores on the ground floor facing Broadway. They completed the building late in the summer of that year and, remembering their native Berlin, named it Unter den Linden. Offering the stores for rent, the Stillgebauers signed a series of ten-year leases with their tenants.

Unter den Linden

In 1901, while most of the block was still vacant, Adolphus Busch bought a major portion of it—the remaining 100 feet along Broadway, extending 175 feet west on 98th Street. He did nothing with the property until 1913, when he and his wife Lilly transferred ownership to the Anheuser-Busch Brewing Association. Under the aegis of his company, Busch erected a small pavillion and opened a summer beer garden, catering to the tastes and habits of the heavily German population that was moving into the neighborhood. His project flourished and he kept it open every summer until the passage of the Volstead Act late in 1919 doomed the venture. Faced with the prospect of Prohibition, Busch sold his land in 1920 to a residential developer, corporately known as the Broadway-98th Street Realty Company. Concurrently, the developer purchased the remaining vacant land along 97th Street from Herman and Frieda Gertner.

Seeking to complete the blockfront, Broadway-98th Street investigated the

127 Essentially vacant except for two ancient frame buildings, the westerly blockfront of Broadway north from 97th Street was still undeveloped when this photograph was made in 1893. A crew of workers are setting a roadway of Belgian blocks—a refined version of cobblestones—while a supply of the granite pavers is piled at the base of the gas streetlamp on the corner. *(Archive of Brown Brothers, courtesy of Henry Collins)*

128 Appearing as one structure, the two fourteen-story apartment houses at 241 West 97th Street and 240 West 98th Street surround the two-story commercial building at the Broadway corner. A full frontage along the avenue would have permitted a more efficient use of the site and would have allowed the builder to construct a single, more visually effective structure instead of two independent ones. The holdout prevented this. *(Andrew Alpern)*

127

128

possibility of acquiring possession of the low 97th Street corner building. The fates had decreed otherwise, however; the timing had been unfortunate.

The Stillgebauers had managed the two-story building carefully, and in the summer of 1909 executed lease documents to keep their building occupied for another ten years. Again, in September and October of 1919 when the second set of leases expired, they had no difficulty in negotiating new ten-year agreements. Able then to offer a predictable cash flow from the building, the family sold it the following month to a group calling itself Purchase Homes Company. Purchase Homes was an investment company and was quite willing to sell its interest in the 97th Street building for a suitable price, but the apartment house developer was deterred by the prospect of having to buy out seven brand-new ten-year store leases. Rather than delay its project and

increase its costs, the developer accepted this ironic twist of fate and constructed the two separate fourteen-story apartment houses that stand today at 241 West 97th Street and 240 West 98th Street, completing them in 1922 (Figure 128). The 98th Street building housed ground floor stores along Broadway, one of which was rented to the original Beefsteak Charlie's chain of restaurants. By a curious coincidence, that lease was assigned in October 1924 to Herman Gertner, who was apparently unable to rid himself of his attachment for that particular block. Mr. Gertner operated the restaurant for a little over a year and then passed it on to the Riverdale Restaurant Corporation.

The stores along Broadway have changed ownership over the years, and the second floor, which housed a synagogue for Austrian Jews for many years, was subsequently occupied by a succession of gypsy fortune-tellers, but the two-

story holdout originally called Unter den Linden remains. Its presence is a reminder of the United States Government's great mistake in thinking it could deprive its citizens of a glass of beer drunk in the cooling shade of a summer garden. The Volstead Act is why the two apartment houses were built, and its timing is why the holdout is still there.

733 Third Avenue

A single holdout can make the development of a new building difficult; two holdouts can mean delays that may threaten the viability of a project; but four holdouts can try the fortitude of even the most patient of developers.

In 1955 Seymour Durst began to assemble the land for what he envisioned as a twenty-four-story office building at Third Avenue and 46th Street to be known as 733 Third Avenue. He needed sixteen parcels for a suitable building, and had no difficulty obtaining fourteen of them, working quietly through agents. He ran into substantial obstacles, however, with the owners of the last two properties, and with tenants in two of the buildings he had already bought.

A Retarded Brother In one old apartment house on the site a middle-aged woman lived with her brother. A relocation expert went to her apartment to discuss her requirements for a new residence, but she refused to let him in. He returned again and again but always the door was barred. He wrote letters and sent telegrams to no avail, and he telephoned. Curiously, the woman was always gracious and courteous on the phone, but she simply refused to let anyone enter her apartment, and would not consider the relocation person's cash offers during six months of attempts at negotiations. A chance remark dropped by a neighbor revealed the reason for the woman's intransigence. She did not want anyone to discover that her brother was retarded, fearing that she would be denied a new apartment because of her brother's condition. Then too, she was reluctant to uproot the unfortunate man from the surroundings he had become accustomed to.

Identifying the problem was half the battle, but even then it took time and persistence to find an apartment in the immediate vicinity that the sister considered suitable.

A Curious Husband In an apartment in another of the doomed buildings on the site lived an elderly and reclusive couple. In their seventies, they seldom left their house except for essential trips to the grocery store. For nearly a year the agents of Mr. Durst tried to talk with them and sensed something strange about their refusal to unlock their apartment door to visitors or to discuss a relocation.

After many months of this frustrating stalemate, the wife was taken ill and went into the hospital where she died within a few days. The surviving spouse then barricaded the door and completely refused to come out, threatening all who attempted conversation. The neighbors became concerned over this behavior and summoned the police. The door was forced and the man was taken away for a psychiatric examination. To everyone's amazement, this revealed that the "husband" was actually a woman. She and her "wife" had lived together for about thirty-five years, and an examination of the apartment turned up a wedding certificate on the wall. Exacerbating the situation, the police then sealed the apartment and began an investigation. They reasoned that the name the "husband" had carried all those years might have belonged to a real man and they wanted to find out what had become of him and whether foul play was involved. Eventually the police surrendered the apartment, the surviving old woman was placed in a nursing home, and the apartment house was vacated.

Sister Catherine's Home Compared with those tenants, the administrators and young working women of Sister Catherine's Home at 212 East 46th Street were quite cooperative, but that didn't mean that the home's building was readied for the bulldozer quickly. It took almost four years of hard bargaining before an agreement was reached on where the young women would live after they left their old abode.

Founded in 1872 by Sister Catherine Jones as a residence for young working women newly arrived in New York, it was originally called The Shelter for Respectable Girls. It moved into the 46th Street building in 1904, and its name was changed after Sister Catherine died. Louise M. Coe, the president of the home's board of trustees, was willing to give up the building the organization had occupied for more than half a century . . . but only if other suitable quarters could be found. Mr. Durst searched out the neighborhood for appropriate buildings and found about a dozen properties from which the trustees could select one which he would acquire for them in exchange for the one they occupied. Ironically, the building which the home finally agreed to accept early in 1959 was one already owned by the Durst firm.

A condition of the exchange was that the new building, at 210 East 49th Street, undergo a complete remodeling, even though it was already in much better condition than the former home. New plumbing, heating, and electrical wiring were installed, and the interior altered and refurbished to meet the needs and desires of the twenty-one girls and two staff members who would live there. Then finally on March 1, 1960, the residents of Sister Catherine's Home moved out, enabling their old building to be razed a few days later in preparation for the excavation of the foundation for the new office structure (Figure 129).

222 East 46th Street One more obstacle remained, however, before construction of 733 Third Avenue could begin. Jack Begelman owned a commercial structure at 222 East 46th Street. The building had been created by combining three nineteenth-century buildings on 46th Street with a one-story backyard brick stable that was equally old (Figure 130). The conversion had been done during the early 1920s and created a single structure shaped like a backwards "L," with the toe formed by the former stable hooking in behind the adjoining lot and sitting right where Mr. Durst wanted to put the corner of his new office building. Mr. Durst offered to buy this 30-foot by 56-foot section of the building, but Mr. Begelman wouldn't even talk about price. He just liked things the way

129

129 The trustees of Sister Catherine's Home held out long after the rest of the block had been demolished. The residents moved only after long negotiations had netted them an alternate building reconstructed to their specifications. *(Courtesy of Real Estate Forum)*

130 Jack Begelman's building at 222 East 46th Street at the time he bought it in 1945. Mr. Begelman replaced the residential tenants with commercial ones and altered the ground floor for an electrical supply store. The holdout portion of the structure, formerly a stable, is hidden behind the old brownstones at the right in the picture. *(Courtesy of The New-York Historical Society)*

130

131 The three giant steel girders positioned over the holdout building to enable 733 Third Avenue to be constructed on top of it and around it. *(Courtesy of* Real Estate Forum*)*

132 One of the three steel columns placed within the Mr. Begelman holdout to support the office building above. In a reversal of the usual procedure, the columns were placed first and then the concrete foundations were poured beneath them. *(Courtesy of* Real Estate Forum*)*

133 The east wall of 733 Third Avenue with the one-time stable in the foreground. The one-story structure extends 50 feet into the envelope of the newer office building—beneath the small-paned windows. *(Andrew Alpern)*

they were and didn't want to make his building any smaller. When months of real estate negotiating proved fruitless, it was an architectural solution that resolved the issue.

Mr. Begelman leased to The Durst Organization the land under his building and the air rights over it, as well as permitting steel columns to be run through the protruding toe of his building to new foundations beneath it. Three giant girders were then erected over the Begelman building to support the office structure above. Each of the girders is 37 feet long, more than 4 feet deep, and weighs 27,000 pounds (Figures 131, 132, and 133). A precedent for this unusual structural feat lies hidden under Times Square. When the original Times Tower was being constructed, the IRT subway had already been built. Since the tracks couldn't be moved, the northeast corner of the Times's building was built both over and under the subway tunnel using similarly large girders to support the load.

With the problem of Jack Begelman's building solved, construction of Mr. Durst's project was able to proceed, and the development was finally completed in 1961, six years after it had been begun (Figure 134). Although it isn't evident from the outside, the floor plan of the second level offices has a corner missing where Mr. Begelman's former stable is engulfed by the new building (Figure 135).

131

132

133

134 Plagued by holdouts, 733 Third Avenue completely surrounds and hides the one that wouldn't succumb. *(Tesla, courtesy of Seymour Durst)*

135 The second floor plan of 733 Third Avenue. The corner cutout accommodates Jack Begelman's holdout structure. The upper floors of 733 are complete rectangles, making use of the air rights leased by Mr. Begelman to the larger building's developer.

134

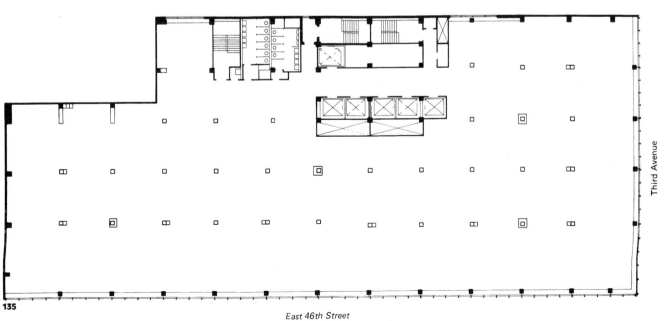

135

East 46th Street

Third Avenue

House of Mansions

136

137

The House of Mansions was designed by Alexander Jackson Davis and erected in 1855 by George Higgins. Taking up the entire easterly blockfront of Fifth Avenue from 41st Street to 42nd Street across from the neo-Egyptian Croton Reservoir, it was a row of eleven individual five-story single-family residences that had been architecturally treated to appear as a single grand gothic-style castellated structure (Figure 136). While other residential rows in New York had received consistent design treatment, this one was the most ambitious and imposing. The separate houses ranged in size from twelve to eighteen rooms apiece and were lavishly planned and decorated. Contemporary advertisements for the houses declared them to be fine, imposing, and of "superior, scientific construction." The views from the upper stories of the houses were asserted to be unrivaled, and to encompass "the Hudson and East rivers, Staten Island, the Palisades, and far into Westchester, and over Long Island."

Despite this hyperbole, and the alleged grandeur of the accommodations, the project was not successful, and five years after it was built, it was purchased by the Rutgers Female Institute (which later moved to New Jersey and became Rutgers College). Conceived as a row of houses, the structure did not conveniently lend itself to conversion as a single integrated building. When vacated by the Rutgers group, it was used ineffectively and uneconomically (Figure 137). The architectural integrity of the House of Mansions was first breached in the early 1880s when the north-moving commercial needs of the city dictated the alteration of the two northernmost houses of the row into facilities for the Bank of Banks, and the demolition of the middle section to provide a site for a new building for the Pottier & Stymus Manufacturing Company's offices.

481 Fifth Avenue By 1892, all that was left of the original block was 481 Fifth Avenue, a narrow remnant of the original grand concept. Complete with its anachronistic front yard, it remained—more a survivor than a holdout—until demolished in 1914 for the new store and office building erected for Rogers Peet & Company (Figure 138).

136 The architect's rendering of the House of Mansions as originally constructed, across from the Croton Reservoir. Appearing as a single structure, it was actually eleven separate row houses. *(Collection of Seymour Durst)*

137 The House of Mansions about 1875 with the old Temple Emanu-El in the background. *(Courtesy of The New-York Historical Society)*

138 The last remaining sliver, representing one-eleventh of the original design of architect A. J. Davis. This scene, captured by the camera in 1892, remained essentially unchanged until 1914 when the last piece of the House of Mansions was demolished. *(Collection of Seymour Durst)*

B. Altman & Company

Benjamin Altman opened a small retail shop at 39 Third Avenue in 1864. By 1876 he had prospered significantly and was widely known as a leader in the dry-goods field, with a flourishing establishment at 19th Street and Sixth Avenue. Presaging the migration of the retail center of trade north from the "Ladies' Mile," Altman began in 1895 to assemble the block at 34th Street and Fifth Avenue for a new store (Figure 139). His first parcel included the 35th Street corner of the block. Six years earlier, the residential character of the neighborhood had been gently disturbed when J. S. A. Griswold sold his house at 355 Fifth Avenue, built originally for Prescott H. Butler, along with his adjoining stable on 34th Street to the art dealer M. Knoedler & Company. Knoedler altered the buildings and reopened them as an art gallery (Figure 140).

By 1904, Mr. Altman had acquired enough property to begin his plans for the new store, designed by architects Trowbridge & Livingston. The building was to be grandly sedate in keeping with the massive marble mansion of merchant A. T. Stewart and the majestic Waldorf-Astoria Hotel across the street. When his new store opened on October 6, 1906, Mr. Altman had still not been able to wrest the 34th Street corner from M. Knoedler & Company. Spurning offers of cash, Knoedler hinted that a long-term lease at favorable rates for a new gallery further uptown might be considered, so Altman bought the northeast corner of 36th Street and Fifth Avenue. On that site was a similarly converted brownstone mansion occupied by the fur salon of C. G. Gunther & Son. However, Knoedler still refused to move (Figure 141).

Mr. Altman retreated, trying to devise a new strategy to dislodge the art dealer, when Knoedler bought a property at 556 Fifth Avenue on its own. The company then erected an elegant new gallery on the midblock site between 45th Street and 46th Street. Later Knoedler abandoned the building to a Schrafft's restaurant and moved to 57th Street, most recently moving again to 70th Street near the Frick Collection.

139

140

141

M. Knoedler & Company vacated the 34th Street house in 1909, and in May 1910 Mr. Altman completed the Fifth Avenue frontage of his store as it had originally been planned (Figures 142 and 143). While the retailer ultimately got what he wanted, Knoedler lost out on the $500,000 Mr. Altman had been prepared to pay as a bonus, and Mr. Altman never again bought anything from the gallery to augment his significant art collection, preferring instead to patronize the establishment of Lord Duveen.

142 The Fifth Avenue façade of B. Altman & Company following its delayed completion. (*Byron, courtesy of the Museum of the City of New York*)

143 The completed Altman's building about 1955 after the removal of the original cornice, belt courses, window enframements, and ionic column capitals. (*Courtesy of B. Altman & Company*)

142

143

592 Eighth Avenue

During the first portion of the nineteenth century, about the best way to avoid the epidemics that periodically plagued New York City was temporarily to move away from the more congested parts of town where the likelihood of contracting the illness was greatest. Thus there was some correlation between the health of New York's residents and the city's real estate development.

In 1829, most of New York's population was clustered near the lower end of Manhattan Island. The Village of Greenwich was a suburb separated from the city by open fields, so when an epidemic of yellow fever struck that year, many New Yorkers fled to that rural area, sparking a frenzy of building activity to accommodate them. A significant number of the modest frame houses hastily erected during that year still exist in Greenwich Village.

Yellow fever struck again in 1853. By that time, however, the Village had become part of the city, and development had moved sufficiently far north to warrant a horse-car route having been extended up Eighth Avenue to 59th Street two years earlier. Anticipating the uptown-directed growth of the city, Thomas Austin had bought the easterly blockfront of Eighth Avenue from 38th Street to 39th Street as soon as the new horse-

car route had been announced. Thinking in a similar fashion, Bradish Johnston bought the land from 37th Street to 38th Street. When the extent of the epidemic became known in 1853, both men recognized the opportunity and erected identical rows of houses for rent to those fleeing the lower portion of the city. Each man divided his blockfront into fifteen lots and each built a row of three-story brick houses, 13 feet 2 inches wide, of simple design (Figure 144).

The Johnston row was sold several times and disappeared completely by 1923, replaced by two large manufacturing loft buildings. Mr. Austin's houses were ultimately sold individually, thus making assemblage of large development sites on that block more difficult.

When John Engelman bought one of the Austin houses at 592 Eighth Avenue in 1922, the entire row was still there—although the two corner houses had been enlarged and two of the midblock ones had been combined and expanded to the rear. The following year, a developer acquired the three houses to the north of Mr. Engelman's as well as a large contiguous parcel on 39th Street. When Mr. Engelman wouldn't sell out, a twenty-story loft building was erected around him.

In 1884, John Gotlieb Wendel bought

144

four houses in the row to add to his already huge portfolio of New York real estate holdings. He had inherited much from his father, including the attitude that real estate was to buy . . . but not to sell. He lived frugally and invested carefully, increasing what he had been given upon his father's death in 1876. When he himself died in 1914, his property went to his sister Ella Von Echtzel Wendel, who continued to inherit more pieces of New York as her sisters died. When Rebecca Wendel Swope—the only one of the family to marry—died in 1930 at the age of 87, Ella V. Wendel had everything, said to be worth $50 million at that time. She died in 1931, still owning every piece of property her family ever bought in America. The following year her holdings on Eighth Avenue were sold to another development group with sights on another loft building project. The group approached John Engelman, but again he wouldn't sell. The loft building went up, as did others on the remainder of the block, until Mr. Engelman's little anachronism was all that remained of Thomas Austin's 1853 response to yellow fever (Figure 145).

By the time John's heir Annette Engelman sold the property in 1961, the building had been extended the full depth of the 64-foot-deep lot and the façade had been altered. But underneath the skin is the mid-nineteenth century structure, hidden from those who pass this peculiarly tenacious holdout.

144 Looking east from Eighth Avenue and 38th Street in 1918. To the left is the most southerly of the fifteen-house row of which holdout 592 Eighth Avenue is the sole survivor. That corner building was enlarged in 1892 when the saloon on the ground floor was installed. To the right is the first of an identical fifteen-house row. Both rows were built in 1853 by different developers. *(Roege, courtesy of The New-York Historical Society)*

145 The 13-foot 2-inch wide three-story building at 592 Eighth Avenue near 39th Street was once one of a row of fifteen identical little brick dwellings erected in 1853. Holdout John Engelman wouldn't sell to successive developers on both sides of his building, and the structure remained in his family until 1961. *(Andrew Alpern)*

145

80 Broad
Street

146

Perhaps the oldest one-family ownership of land in all New York, and certainly the most tenacious of all holdouts, is the 15-foot-wide building site on Broad Street at the northwest corner of Stone Street. The land was bought in 1720 by Augustus Jay, whose grandson John Jay later became the first Chief Justice of the United States Supreme Court. It was improved with a succession of modest buildings, altered or replaced as the changing needs of the area dictated. The deed was passed from one family member to another, with the tradition of not selling or mortgaging the land developing slowly until it was codified in the will of Peter Augustus Jay who died in 1843. He wrote,

I give and devise to my son, Peter Augustus Jay and his heirs my lot or parcel of land in the City of New York, bounded easterly in front by Broad Street, southerly by Stone Street, and northerly by land of my brother William Jay. I have neither the power nor the intention to render the parcel of property above devised inalienable, but there are recollections and circumstances connected with it which make me desirous that it should remain in the family. The lot in Broad Street was purchased by my great grandfather about 1720 and was the first land owned by our family in America. I earnestly request my son not to sell or mortgage this land.

88 Broad Street During this century, until 1929, the 88 Broad Street site was occupied by a five-story tenement house. It was not able to support itself financially, the $4000 annual tax bill alone being more than the rent roll, so the building was taken down and a three-story commercial structure that was expected to produce a greater cash flow was erected. Shortly thereafter, the Maritime Association made vigorous efforts to acquire the site to complete its assemblage for a new office building to be known as 80 Broad Street. Notwithstanding the stock market crash and the ensuing depression, the Jay family heirs abided by their ancestor's wishes and declined the inflated offers of the association.

Thwarted in its attempts to obtain the entire blockfront, the Maritime Association elected to develop as much of the plottage as it owned, turning to builder Abraham N. Adelson to construct the building. Sloan & Robertson was the architectural design firm for the thirty-seven-story structure, which was completed in 1931 (Figure 146).

The building at 88 Broad Street is now occupied by a small restaurant and a furniture showroom (Figure 147). While the tenancy may change and the building be altered or replaced, the Jay family is still producing sons and is totally committed to maintaining the continuous ownership under the Jay name that was begun by Augustus Jay more than 260 years ago.

147

146 At thirty-seven stories and 320,000 square feet, 80 Broad Street towers over the little three-story structure occupying the venerable holdout site at 88 Broad on the corner of Stone Street. *(Jay Berman, courtesy of Edward S. Gordon Company)*

147 The bulk of the adjacent office building looms over 88 Broad Street, whose site has been held by the Jay family since 1720—a holdout against all blandishments. *(Andrew Alpern)*

Citicorp Center

When one of the largest banks in the country decides it wants to build a major building on almost a full city block, it is axiomatic that the assemblage of the needed land must be done in a way that will keep the bank's involvement secret. This is to diminish the likelihood of one of the landowners sniffing a captive and rich buyer and holding out for an outrageous price. But even with the identity of the true developer a secret, holdout situations can develop that might try the patience and resources of the most seasoned real estate person.

The acquisition of the block from 53rd Street to 54th Street on Lexington Avenue for development as the Citicorp Center (Figure 148) was carried on in the customary cloak-and-dagger manner, but nonetheless it took five years and $40 million to secure the property, and in the process several difficult holdouts emerged. Curiously, the building that today represents what appears to be the major holdout against the Citicorp project in the eyes and minds of most passers-by, was never a holdout at all. Rather, it was the spark that started the entire development idea.

St. Peter's Church The project began in 1968 when the congregation of St. Peter's Lutheran Church sat down to consider what to do about its faltering financial condition. In 1871 St. Peter's had bought an old church building at 46th Street and Lexington Avenue for $45,000. By 1902 the area had become primarily commercial and the value of the land under their church had increased significantly. When approached by the New York Central Railroad, the congregation was happy to accept $200,000 for the 46th Street plot, and with the money it built a new home in a residential location at 54th Street and Lexington Avenue. By the mid-1960s, commerce had again caught up with St. Peter's, making the sale of its church and a relocation to a smaller building at a less expensive site a solution to the congregation's problems (Figure 149).

Hearing about the overtures St. Peter's had made to find a suitable alternative location, real estate brokers Donald Schnabel and Charles McArthur thought that with the church property as a nucleus they could assemble sufficient land on the block to interest some developer who might want to erect an office building. With its corporate headquarters directly across the street, an obvious possibility was the First National City Bank Corporation (now Citicorp). Messrs. Schnabel and McArthur ap-

149

proached the bank cold, and after several months of meetings it agreed to retain the brokers' firm of Julien J. Studley Inc. to assemble the necessary land (Figures 150, 151, and 152).

148 Citicorp Center as ultimately built. *(Howard Associates, courtesy of W. Easley Hamner and Hugh Stubbins & Associates)*

149 The 1903 St. Peter's Church just prior to its demolition. Behind it is the brick bulk of the Medical Chambers holdout building of 1930. *(Andres Küng, courtesy of Mildred Westermann and St. Peter's Church)*

150 The Lexington Avenue end of the Citicorp Center site before demolition began. The original St. Peter's Church is at the left. *(Courtesy of Donald Schnabel)*

151 Third Avenue from 53rd to 54th Streets as it appeared before the Citicorp Center changed its appearance. The 880 Third Avenue office building is at the left. *(Courtesy of Donald Schnabel)*

152 Typical of many one-family brownstone houses built in the 1880s, these two on East 53rd Street were part of the Citicorp assemblage. *(Courtesy of Donald Schnabel)*

150

151

152

The Studley firm set up several straw companies to serve as conduits for the property transfers, and began its work of acquiring all the needed parcels. Broker Schnabel began with 139 East 53rd Street, a small four-story building with the haute cuisine Café Chauveron on its ground floor. A single meeting with Roger Chauveron and his partner determined that the restaurant's lease could be bought out for $300,000. Buying the building itself was not so simple.

Manny Duell Manny Duell was a sometimes-developer who played at being a professional holdout in his spare time. He had somehow sniffed out a possible assemblage on the block and had signed purchase contracts with the owners of the Chauveron building and the ones on both sides of it. Mr. Schnabel dickered for several weeks with Mr. Duell, who wanted to find out who was behind the broker with the money. They came to an agreement without the bank's identity being revealed, however, and on August 13, 1969, the deal was consummated. Mr. Duell received $2.3 million for the rights to purchase the three properties. He had held the contracts for less than three months and had put down a tiny fraction of the amount he realized from the deal. With the bank's money, Mr. Schnabel had paid $430 per square foot—just for the right to buy the first three parcels; the owners still had to be paid for the deeds. But in the process he had extracted from the cagey Mr. Duell a guarantee not to make further attempts to thwart the assemblage.

Eva Trefner The next brief holdout came in the form of a warmhearted woman named Eva Trefner, who had run, for more than twenty years, a modest Hungarian restaurant at 619 Lexington Avenue near the corner of 53rd Street. She was reluctant to sell out because it would put "her people" out of work, the waiters and busboys who had been with her so many years. With the assurance from Mr. Schnabel that the restaurant could remain open for at least a year to give all her employees the opportunity to find new jobs, Mrs. Trefner agreed to sell for $400,000. And with a significant portion of the proceeds, she rewarded her faithful staff, including $25,000 for her longtime chef.

Thomas Howard For a basically commercial midtown block, there were a surprising number of residential occupants, both owners and renters. One particularly tough challenge was Thomas Howard, an elderly bachelor who had lived for twenty-two years in the brownstone house he owned at 150 East 54th Street. "They'll carry me out of here in a box," he said to Mr. Schnabel's partner, Charles McArthur.

Mr. Howard was not in good health and he seldom left his house. With no dependents and sufficient independent income to take care of his wants, he had no reason to sell. But he was a lonely man, so he welcomed Mr. McArthur's visits. "Come often, Charlie," he said, "as long as it's only social. Because I'm never going to sell."

While dealing with Mr. Howard in an effort to wear down his resolve, Mr. McArthur negotiated a lease buy-out with the ground floor tenant, a small clothing shop. Then he continued gently to press his quest with Mr. Howard for two years. Feeling that the holdout impasse had lasted long enough, Mr. McArthur proffered a contract with the purchase price missing. He told Howard to fill in a final price within forty-eight hours for an immediate decision. Howard wrote in $815,000—$427 a square foot—and his price was accepted.

A Religious Man Another reluctant resident on the site lived in a rooming house where he paid $8 a week for a single small room. He asserted that he wouldn't move until God told him to do so. When Mr. Schnabel sent a $500 donation to the man's church in his name, the little holdout decided that God had spoken the right words and he moved.

Two Old Sisters Two other residents of the block were Julia and Alyce Belora, a pair of frail sisters in their eighties. They agreed to move without a penny in direct payment, but with a touch of luxury they had never known. When they said that they would move to California to live with their sister if they had to leave their apartment, Mr. Schnabel sent a particularly solicitous moving company to pack and ship their belongings. He then sent a private limousine to drive them to the airport and provided first class plane tickets to the coast. The two old ladies thoroughly enjoyed the celebrity treatment and even sent a thank-you note from their new home.

Medical Chambers The longest holdout on the block, and perhaps the most difficult, was the Medical Chambers. Built as a cooperative venture forty years earlier, the thirteen-story structure was owned jointly by forty prosperous doctors who maintained their offices in the building (Figure 153). At first Donald Schnabel approached the group's board of directors with an offer to exchange their building for a bigger one, reno-

vated to suit their needs. The doctors' answer was to dismiss their board for even discussing the matter. With a new board in place, Mr. Schnabel found his next offer of $4 million cash also rejected. To an offer of a brand new building constructed to their specifications, the doctors also said no.

The negotiations went on for more than three years before a solution was developed that would enable the doctors to make a significant profit from the sale of their building without losing much of it to taxes. Since both Citicorp and Medical Chambers were stock companies, a merger was devised in which the Chambers' corporation became a subsidiary of the bank, and each doctor received $24 of Citicorp stock for each $1 of Medical Chambers stock he held. The merger was registered with the Securities and Exchange Commission and enabled the doctors to defer payment of their capital gains taxes on the transaction until they individually chose to sell their newly acquired bank stock. In October 1973, 3½ years after Mr. Schnabel had first approached them, the doctors vacated Medical Chambers. Since right to the end there was a strong possibility that something might go awry, Hugh Stubbins and Associates, the bank's architects, prepared a complete set of plans for an alternative, smaller building whose site excluded the Chambers' land. Luckily, that scheme never had to be used.

Carroll's Pub and Howard Johnson's There were two other holdouts which had an effect on the architects' planning of the new building. At the corner of Lexington Avenue and 53rd Street the ground floor was occupied by a Howard Johnson's coffee shop, and two doors farther north on Lexington Avenue was Carroll's Pub (Figure 154). Both establishments were merely tenants, since Citicorp had already bought the deeds to their buildings. But both places were equally determined not to move until their leases expired. Although negotiations continued (and were eventually to be successful), the architects were instructed to consider that the two holdout buildings would be reduced to one-story height and to plan the new office tower around them. The Citicorp Center that was actually built reflects this; had the two holdouts remained to the end of their lease periods, only the entrance plaza to the new building would have been affected, and then only temporarily.

Even with all the other needed properties on the block secured, a deal had to be struck with St. Peter's—the original impetus for the entire project. The

153 The Medical Chambers building on East 54th Street. The tenaciousness of its doctor-owners in holding out against Citicorp forced the architects of the project to design a lesser tower as a fall-back position in case the Medical Chambers plot could not be acquired. *(Courtesy of Donald Schnabel)*

154 Carroll's Pub and Howard Johnson's leased ground-floor space in separate buildings on Lexington Avenue. Citicorp acquired the deeds to the buildings but had great difficulty in buying out the leases of the two tenants. The positioning of the Citicorp Center on its site reflects the possibility that the two holdouts might have remained long after construction of the new tower had begun. *(Courtesy of W. Easley Hamner and Hugh Stubbins & Associates)*

153

154

congregation was quite willing to sell, since its existing quarters weren't at all satisfactory for its current purposes. The group retained John White of the real estate consulting firm of James D. Landauer Associates to search out an appropriate alternative midtown site, but nothing suitable could be found. St. Peters' pastor, the Reverend Ralph E. Peterson, together with Messrs. White and Schnabel, needed to devise a way that Citicorp could get its building while St. Peter's could still have a church.

The solution came in the form of a condominium arrangement in which the church would have its own identity in the form of a new building on essentially the same spot it had occupied before. By being a condominium partner with the bank, rather than its tenant, the church was able to avoid having to pay real estate taxes on its land. Through the condominium, the church and the bank were able to share portions of the project as "common elements," to their mutual advantage. For its part, Citicorp constructed the shell of the new church building—enclosing 40,000 square feet of space—and gave the congregation $9 million. Although St. Peter's had hoped that the sum would give it a substantial endowment, by the time the project was complete, it had all been spent. The congregation, however, had traded its 15,000 square foot site for a permanent home responsive to its needs (Figure 155). And Citicorp obtained its new headquarters building in a sympathetic setting, ecumenically joining God and mammon to the benefit of both.

A Holdout Within a Holdout The Citicorp Center occupies almost the entire block. Only 880 Third Avenue—an office building—remains from before. As a large, comparatively modern structure, its acquisition cost was simply more than the Citicorp project could handle. A holdout in its own right, it encompasses another holdout within itself. When 880 was built, the nineteenth-century tenement house on the corner of 53rd Street couldn't be bought, so the new structure had to be built around it (Figure 156). Several years later, the owners of the office tower were finally able to acquire the former holdout. They demolished it and replaced it with an addition to the larger building, constructed with a matching façade (Figures 157 and 158).

155

156

155 The 54th Street façade of the new St. Peter's Church designed by Hugh A. Stubbins, Jr. Occupying the same site as its predecessor, the church and its congregation obtained additional usable space through a condominium arrangement with Citicorp Center. *(John Stevens Kerr, courtesy of Mildred Westermann and St. Peter's Church)*

156 The holdout at 876 Third Avenue at the northwest corner of the avenue's intersection with 53rd Street. Most of Third Avenue was lined with five-story buildings such as this until the demolition of the elevated train tracks brought progress and development. This one wouldn't be bought out and forced the developer of 880 Third Avenue to build his new office building around it. *(Courtesy of The Durst Organization)*

157 When the corner holdout finally succumbed, the owners of 880 Third Avenue rebuilt the site for an addition to the surrounding building. *(Douglas A. Kreeger)*

158 The only building on the block which antedates the Citicorp Center is 880 Third Avenue. A holdout in its own right, it contains the ghost of the earlier corner holdout, clearly evident from the discontinuity of the structure. *(Andrew Alpern)*

157

158

342 Madison Avenue

When a holdout building owner stands pat and the developer of the adjoining site must build around the holdout, more likely than not the building causing the trouble is an important corner. Examples are P. J. Clarke's at 55th Street and Third Avenue, the building now housing Nedicks at 34th Street and Broadway, and the Hurley's Tavern structure at 49th Street and Sixth Avenue.

How unusual, then, to find a builder who built around *two* holdout buildings—and ones that were right in the middle of his site, at that (Figure 159). Builder Frank Colburn Pinkham got his new building for the Canadian-Pacific Railroad in 1921 despite the two small old ones that wouldn't sell, but he had to settle for a peculiarly contorted structure (Figure 160).

It is an accepted truism that a simple rectangular shape is the most economical one for an office building, since it best lends itself to subdivision for its occupants, and there is a minimum amount of perimeter wall to construct. Over the years this means that there is that much less exterior envelope to maintain, and that much less area through which heat

159 The demolition of St. Bartholomew's Church in preparation for the construction of 342 Madison Avenue. The two holdout buildings are the second and fourth ones from the left. *(Byron, courtesy of the Museum of the City of New York)*

160 The completed structure at 342 Madison Avenue when it was known as the Canadian Pacific Building. Visible are the two original holdout buildings. *(Byron, courtesy of the Museum of New York)*

159

can be lost. But because of the two hold-outs, the shape of 342 Madison Avenue is an uneconomical, inefficient, mis-formed capital "E" (Figure 161). The two roadblocks to economical design were the

336 and 340 Madison Avenue four-story former residence at 336 Madison Avenue and the six-story building at 340 Madison of Pease & Elliman (Figure 162), a now-defunct real estate firm that should have known better. The recalcitrance of their owners has re-sulted in a floor plan that is a nightmare to space planners who attempt to create layouts of even moderate efficiency.

The architects of 342 Madison Ave-nue, A. D. Pickering and Starrett & Van Vleck, integrated facilities for the Fifth Church of Christ, Scientist into the new building, thereby perpetuating the re-ligious use of the property established by St. Bartholomew's Church that had formerly occupied a portion of the site.

A few years after the completion of 342 Madison, John Dilliard rebuilt the two holdout structures, using H. Craig Severance as architect for the southerly one and Joseph H. Freedlander for the other (Figure 163). Ironically, they are now interconnected at each floor with 342, and form a part of it (Figure 164).

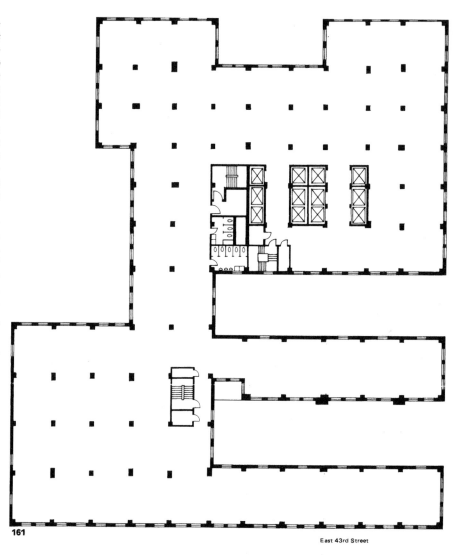

161

East 43rd Street

161 A plan of a typical floor at 342 Madison Ave-nue. The two holdouts have given it the awkward E-shape. *(Courtesy of Brefries Madison Associates)*

162 The building of the real estate firm of Pease & Elliman at 340 Madison Avenue that Frank Col-burn Pinkham couldn't buy, c. 1910. At the right is the rectory of St. Bartholomew's Church. *(Wurts, courtesy of the Museum of the City of New York)*

163 The National American Building that re-placed the original holdout at 340 Madison Avenue in 1928. Its floors were constructed to align with those of the adjacent office building. *(Wurts, cour-tesy of the Museum of the City of New York)*

164 342 Madison Avenue in a recent photo-graph showing the two small buildings that re-placed the original two holdouts. They have been integrated internally with the larger structure. *(An-drew Alpern)*

162

163

The Spite House

Many building lots in New York antedate the mapping of the adjoining streets, so when those streets were cut through, odd-shaped parcels were left over. It wasn't until the 1870s that upper Lexington Avenue came into being, and when it was laid out, a narrow piece of land at the northwest corner of the new avenue and 82nd Street was left over. It was 102 feet long but only 5 feet wide, so it appeared not to have much use.

It was part of a large parcel of land that had been assembled by Thomas W. McLeay and inherited by his wife Emma Jane when he died in 1865. In 1881 the skinny site was bought by Emily Emmett, along with two more conventionally shaped adjoining lots. Although Emmett's name appears on the deed, the actual owner was her uncle, Joseph Richardson. Mr. Richardson was a building contractor, a sometimes-developer, and a real estate manipulator who considered it prudent to keep many of his assets in the names of various relatives. He executed projects for the Vanderbilt and Gould families, and was responsible for constructing the expansion of the original Grand Central Depot. Within the context of the normal business practices of that time, his actions in concealing assets from potential creditors were not especially unusual.

It is not known which was the outgrowth of the other, but besides indirectly buying Emma McLeay's land in 1881, Mr. Richardson became engaged to her the same year. Early in 1882 they were married, and concurrently Mr. Richardson's eccentric behavior gained him a curious notoriety.

Patrick McQuade intended to build a pair of walk-up apartment houses on land he owned on 82nd Street directly adjacent to Mr. Richardson's 5-foot strip on Lexington. He felt that it would be more profitable if one of his houses could enjoy the benefits of a corner location. He assumed that nothing could be built on the left-over 5 feet, so he offered $1000 for the strip—$200 less than the figure at which the city had assessed it. Mr. Richardson was said to have had more grandiose ideas, and to have held out for $5000, a price Mr. McQuade was unwilling to pay.

Undaunted, Mr. McQuade hired Alfred B. Ogden to design his apartment buildings, including windows on the lot line under the assumption that Mr. Richardson's lot would forever remain vacant. Construction of the pair of buildings began on May 22, 1882, triggering Richardson's spitefulness. Fresh from having just completed the construction of a marble-fronted row of one-family residences nearby, he returned to the drafting board and less than a month later, filed plans for a pair of buildings of his own, each 51 feet long, on the Lexington Avenue lot. While each house was nominally only 5 feet wide, advantage was taken of a clause in the New York City building regulations that permitted corner houses to have bay window extensions. This enabled the main rooms on each floor to be a little over seven feet wide (Figure 165). Since the Richardson buildings were much smaller than those of Mr. McQuade, they took less effort to construct, and were completed in November 1882, almost five months earlier than the side-street houses (Figures 166 and 167). Perhaps exhausted from the battle with Richardson, Mr. McQuade sold the apartment houses on September 1, 1884, to Hyman Sarner, a local clothier.

While Richardson must have been a trifle odd to have built such a pair of houses just for spite, he proved himself even stranger, because he actually moved into one of them and lived in it. He rented the other out to a succession of tenants at $500 a year. Furnishing a house as narrow as Richardson's required specially made furniture, the dining table being only 18 inches wide and the chairs proportionately small. The kitchen stove was the smallest the manufacturer had ever constructed, and the beds were barely wide enough to hold their occupants. Their staircase and halls were too narrow to permit two people to pass, and for some they weren't even wide enough for one. The story is told that Deacon Terry, a reporter for *The American*, was sent to the house one summer day during the early 1890s to interview Mr. Richardson and got stuck in the winding staircase. Despite the efforts of neighbors to push him one way or the other, the broad-girthed Mr. Terry remained firmly wedged in. Only by

165 This drawing and floor plan of Joseph Richardson's unusual house at 1216 Lexington Avenue clearly show how the building was divided into two separate dwellings. Although the lot was 5 feet wide, the usable space inside the wall construction was only 3 feet 4 inches wide, so three bays were included to bring the width of those rooms to a relatively spacious 7 feet 3 inches. In those days, such encroachments on the public sidewalks were not prohibited. These drawings were published in the January 1887 issue of *Scientific American*. *(Courtesy of The New-York Historical Society)*

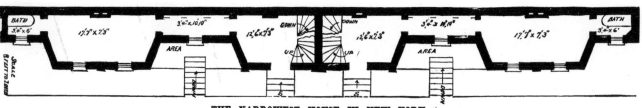

THE NARROWEST HOUSE IN NEW YORK.

166 The Spite House about 1895 during construction work along Lexington Avenue. The white building directly to the north on the avenue was also constructed by Mr. Richardson and still exists. *(Collection of Andrew Alpern)*

167 These drawings of Joseph Richardson and the house he built on his 5-foot strip of land were made to illustrate an article telling of his final illness in the *New York Journal,* June 5, 1897. *(Courtesy of The New-York Historical Society)*

THE DINING ROOM

JOSEPH RICHARDSON

"THE HOUSE OF SPITE"

Dying Millionaire Richardson and the Strange House He Lives In.

167

wriggling out of his clothes was he able to extricate himself, and he finished the interview on the roof in his shorts.

Having arrived in New York from his native England in 1833, Mr. Richardson forged a successful career as a contractor and accumulated significant wealth in the process. Despite this, he was frugal in the extreme and went to great lengths to conserve his funds. For years he carried his lunch to work with him in a paper bag (reused until it wore out), and Richardson himself confirmed that he had once persuaded a physician to halve his bill, much in the manner of the infamous multimillionaire Hetty Green, by disguising himself in the raiment of a hod carrier and pleading poverty.

Joseph and Emma Richardson were content to live in the Spite House, but Dellaripha Richardson, Joseph's daughter by his first wife, refused to visit it, declaring that it was "too swell" for her tastes. She preferred to remain where she had long lived in a dwelling on East Houston Street called by her neighbors "the Prison House." Reflecting her father's penchant for odd behavior, she was seen by the neighbors only in the early morning, when she swept the steps, visited the grocery store for some bare necessities, and returned to immure herself behind barred windows, where she refused to see any visitors.

The daughter was as avaricious and parsimonious as the father, and after his death in 1897, she brought suit to contest the will which gave her stepmother a portion of her father's estate. Joseph Richardson's holdings were said to have been worth something between $4 million and $30 million, but little could be located. Dellaripha herself refused to turn over to the Surrogate's Court some strongboxes of her father's she had been keeping, and did so only when threatened with jail. When the boxes were opened, the bonds they were supposed to have contained had vanished. Other assets similarly disappeared, showing up later in her vault and that of her brother George. When the legal battle over the will was finally resolved and the document admitted to probate two years later, barely enough cash was realized to pay the $50,000 legacy Mr. Richardson had left to his Baptist pastor, the $17,500 he left to pay off the mortgage on his church, and to reimburse the $200,000 his widow asserted she had spent on legal fees.

Emma Richardson was not finished fighting with her stepdaughter, however. In August of 1900 and again the following November, Dellaripha brought a claim against her stepmother in an attempt to dispossess her from the Spite House so it could be sold for the daughter's benefit. Although Joseph Richardson had transferred ownership of the Spite House to his wife in 1892, in 1896 he gave his daughter a deed to the same property. Thinking she owned the building, Dellaripha claimed the old woman was merely a tenant-at-will and could be evicted. The judge who dismissed the suits expressed regret that he couldn't find some harsher way to deal with the difficult stepdaughter.

Mr. Richardson's Spite House cramped his neighbor's building, and was a local landmark for more than thirty years, but in September of 1915 it vanished, a victim of progress. The real estate development firm of Bing and Bing bought the Richardson property as well as the adjacent Sarner houses and tore them down to make room for a newer and larger apartment house (Figure 168). Mr. Richardson's adjoining marble-fronted row remains, however, converted to stores on the ground floor with apartments above.

168 In 1904, Mr. Richardson's widow sold the Spite House, perhaps anticipating her death three years later. The new owner bricked up the end windows and converted the ground floor for use as a tailoring shop. This photograph was taken in 1912, a little more than two years before the building was taken down. *(Public Service Commission, courtesy of The New-York Historical Society)*

The Sulgrave

In 1921, the builder/developer firm of Klein and Jackson planned a residential hotel at 60 East 67th Street. The firm had acquired 80 feet of frontage on the side street, but lacked the final 20 feet necessary to give it the desirable Park Avenue corner. The obstacle came in the form of Sophia T. Hawkins, who owned the house on the corner. An active woman in her mid-80s with strongly held opinions and the financial means to support them, she was the widow of Dexter A. Hawkins. Her husband had been equally outspoken, vigorously espousing compulsory public education in the 1870s and loudly lobbying for its support in Albany. Mrs. Hawkins had more than enough money to live comfortably, and had no intention of quitting the house she had called her home for so many years. The builder's offers were pointedly ignored.

Sophia T Hawkins

Plans proceeded without the holdout site, and drawings for the new building were prepared by the architectural firm of Rouse and Goldstone. Construction began, and the hotel was completed in 1923 (Figure 169). Shortly after The Sulgrave opened, however, its owners seized upon an opportunity to expand onto Park Avenue, just to the south of Mrs. Hawkins's house.

In 1905 646 Park Avenue had been erected on the site of two earlier brownstone residences. It was built by Susan Dows Herter as an eight-story facility for the Charlton School. When Charlton no longer needed it, the building was sold, and in the fall of 1917, the newly formed Lincoln School opened, occupying the entire building. In the spring of 1922, the school relocated to new quarters on Morningside Heights as part of the Columbia University Teachers College which had been instrumental in its establishment. The building was then sold to the corporation which owned the apartment house adjoining it at 640 Park Avenue. Perhaps the company had ideas of operating the two buildings as one, but such a plan never came to fruition and on February 24, 1924, title to 646 passed to The Sulgrave. The hotel made the necessary alterations and then operated the structure as an annex to its main building around the corner. A few years later, the hotel also acquired the row house adjoining it at 50 East 67th Street, converting the little building to fifteen additional hotel rooms.

In 1929, Mrs. Hawkins died at the age of 92, and on June 15, 1930, title to her house was conveyed to The Sulgrave's owners. Rather than converting the house to yet more rooms, the hotel's management elected to demolish it, constructing in its stead a formal garden terrace on which meals were served alfresco from the restaurant in the hotel

169 The home of Mrs. Dexter A. Hawkins at the corner of 67th Street and Park Avenue about 1928. The refusal of Mrs. Hawkins to sell her house kept the adjoining Sulgrave Hotel from fronting on Park Avenue. *(Percy C. Byron, courtesy of the Museum of the City of New York)*

170

(Figure 170). The owners had apparently overextended themselves, however, for in December of 1931, the entire assemblage of buildings along with the terrace was sold at a foreclosure auction for $5000 more than the outstanding debt of $1.4 million.

In 1956, a later owner erected a two-story restaurant structure on the terrace site, but only four years later the entire hotel site was sold to an investing group which demolished the entire accretion of buildings. Plans were drawn by the architectural firm of Emery Roth & Sons for a twenty-one-story building with sixty-three apartment units, but this project was never built. The property was subsequently acquired by the self-made Greek immigrant developer/builder John Kokkins who paid $4 million for the site. Ignoring the dignified atmosphere of Park Avenue, Mr. Kokkins erected a harshly angled and starkly white twenty-one-story cooperative apartment house, completing it in 1963. An article in *The New York World Telegram and Sun* at the time described the structure as being especially well designed and constructed. However, when compared to the substantial limestone and red brick structures of its immediate surroundings, its glazed façade and bright aluminum window frames give it a singularly inappropriate and cheap appearance among its older and more refined neighbors (Figure 171).

171

170 The Sulgrave corner about 1946 after the Hawkins holdout had been replaced with a dining terrace serving the hotel's restaurant. At the left is 646 Park Avenue, a turn-of-the-century school building which later provided additional rooms for The Sulgrave. *(William Henry, courtesy of Donald Weill)*

171 The intrusive apartment block that obliterated all traces of Mrs. Hawkins's house and The Sulgrave Hotel against which she had held out. *(Lloyd Acker, courtesy of The New York Public Library)*

Seven Park Avenue

Although most New York City architecture is relatively anonymous-looking and goes through its life in an uneventful manner, once in a while a building is encountered which is distinctive in appearance and which attains a notoriety not ordinarily expected.

During the 1840s, the residential development of Manhattan Island was geographically spread out, but was gradually working its way farther and farther north. Much of the land was still considered to be out in the country, and the design of many of the buildings reflected this.

One of the buildings erected at this time was constructed on the northeast corner of 34th Street and Park Avenue (then known as Fourth Avenue). It was 2½ stories high, compact, and, as befitted a house that was several miles north of the center of the city, it had been ornamented with gables and gingerbread fretwork at the eaves reminiscent of the little carpenter-gothic cottages to be found in the villages of upstate New York. The entrance was at the top of a long flight of steps—the traditional New York stoop—and the house was set back from the street behind an iron fence and a yard of grass and trees (Figure 172).

Adjoining the house to the east were two small carriage houses, each modest and unassuming. About 1869 these were replaced with a matched pair of four-story row houses with mansard roofs. Then in 1882 the cottage on the corner

172 The Bacon house holdout in its original form. The picture was published about 1865 as a stereograph by the E. & H. T. Anthony Company. The brownstone row houses adjoining the 1840s gothic revival cottage were no more than six or eight years old when this photograph was taken. *(Courtesy of Frederick S. Lightfoot, Benjamin Blom, and Dover Publications)*

173

174

173 The Bacon house about 1908 when its address was One Park Avenue. Even then—before it was a holdout—it looked at the least like a survivor from an earlier and perhaps gentler time, with its curious gables, gingerbread, and large front yard. *(Collection of Andrew Alpern)*

174 The imminent destruction of the living room mantel in the nineteenth-century Bacon house holdout. *(Nat Fein for* The New York Herald Tribune, *courtesy of Seymour Durst)*

175 The northeast corner of 34th Street and Park Avenue in 1952 with the two sections of the apartment house at Seven Park Avenue separated by Mrs. Robert Bacon's holdout. *(Lloyd Acker, courtesy of The New York Public Library)*

176 The northeast corner of 34th Street and Park Avenue with the Bacon house replaced by an extension of Seven Park Avenue to fill in the corner plot. *(Andrew Alpern)*

was enlarged considerably, although the exterior style of the house retained the finials, fretwork, and other gothic detailing of the original cottage. In 1899, the building's owner, Robert W. Bacon, bought the pair of adjoining row houses and integrated them with the corner structure to form a residence of impressive size (Figure 173). He retained the architectural firm of Howard Cauldwell & Morgan to make façade changes to complement the other work it had done to the augmented Bacon home. Inside, the house was completely redecorated in suitably grandiose style with elaborate paneling, stained glass, and carved fireplace mantels (Figure 174).

When Fourth Avenue north of 34th Street was renamed Park Avenue, the corner house became known as number one. Shortly after, Commodore Cornelius Vanderbilt erected his new Grand Central Depot at 42nd Street, sparking heavy development in the Murray Hill area surrounding the quaint old house at 34th Street. Carefully maintained fol-

175

176

lowing its successive enlargements, the house and its neighbors changed little until the early 1920s.

In 1924, the real estate developer Henry Mandel bought the former horse-car stables at Fourth Avenue and 32nd Street. He announced that he would build an eighteen-story office building on the site if the city would extend the name of Park Avenue two blocks south and give his proposed building the fashionable address of One Park Avenue. The city said it would comply, but it hadn't reckoned on Mrs. Bacon, who still lived in the house at 34th Street. Colonel and Mrs. Bacon had enjoyed the prestige of dwelling at One Park Avenue for many years, and Mrs. Bacon was not about to give it up without a fight. She took her case through two levels of appeal to the highest court in New York State before she was finally defeated. Her husband, a former secretary of state and ambassador to France, wasn't there to share her disappointment, however, having died five years earlier.

Until her own death in 1940, Mrs. Bacon managed to retain her telephone directory listing as One Park Avenue, but otherwise gave her address as "Park Avenue at 34th Street Northeast." A small sign affixed to her home gave that information to passers-by.

Mrs. Robert Bacon While her holdout against the change in house numbering was not successful, Mrs. Bacon had more luck in resisting a real estate developer who wanted to build a large apartment house at 34th Street and Park Avenue. Vivian Green had acquired 23 feet along Park Avenue and 83 feet on 34th Street in 1929, but he lacked the corner lot he needed to erect a suitable building. Try as he would, Mrs. Bacon refused to yield to his blandishments, so he was forced to construct a compromise building, completing it early in 1931 (Figure 175). While the first floor lobby is connected, above that level the building was actually two separate structures. The section on 34th Street was

designed like a conventional side-street building with ten very small apartments per floor, while the Park Avenue section had room for only two units at each story. The discontinuity of the two sections forced architect Emery Roth to provide double the number of fire stairs and double the number of elevators that would otherwise have been required. Naturally, the added construction costs imposed on developer Green by Mrs. Bacon's refusal to sell were passed on to the building's tenants in the form of higher rents.

Following the death of the old woman, the house remained boarded up while the estate was settled and a disputed mortgage lien held by the Equitable Life Assurance Society cleared. Then in 1953 it was finally taken down, and in its place an extension to Seven Park Avenue was constructed, adding four more apartments to each floor and filling in the corner to form a semblance of what Mr. Green had had in mind a quarter of a century before (Figure 176).

Mayfair House

In the 1880s, following the completion of Cornelius Vanderbilt's Grand Central Depot and the lowering below grade of the tracks for his New York Central Railroad, residential development along Park Avenue began. Because the smoke-belching trains ran in an open cut, lot lines were altered so the houses could be oriented toward the side streets. Along the south side of East 65th Street, a long row of 20-foot-wide brownstones was erected; the last was number 64 at the corner of Park Avenue. The building's long side paralleled the avenue, and at the rear of the lot about midway between 64th Street and 65th Street, there was a small backyard garden.

When Clara Bowron bought the house in 1912, she felt that the garden's frontage on Park Avenue could be put to better use, so she erected a small garage on the site with two floors of servants' living quarters above. In 1921 she added a fourth floor to the little building, and then the following year she converted the structure into a small self-contained house, commissioning architect Joel D.

608 Park Avenue Barber to design the present façade, and giving it the address of 608 Park Avenue (Figure 177).

It appears that she did this in anticipation of selling her larger house on the corner to the developers of Mayfair House, an apartment hotel whose builders had already acquired a sizable site on 65th Street. Where the stubborn refusal of Sophia Hawkins to yield the corner two blocks further north to a different set of apartment-hotel developers frustrated the plans of their architect, Clara Bowron's flexibility enabled her to remain on at least a portion of her property while Mayfair House was given the prestigious corner to develop. The larger building was completed in 1925 at 610 Park Avenue with a brick and limestone façade that is sympathetic to its little neighbor (Figure 178). Number 608 remained Clara Bowron's home until her death in 1947. Her estate then sold the house to the Kingdom of Sweden which uses it as the residence of a high-ranking member of its delegation to the United Nations.

177 The substantial width and four stories of 608 Park Avenue belie its diminutive size; it is built only 20 feet deep behind its stripped-down neo-Georgian façade. To the right, and looming up behind it, is the fifteen-story Mayfair House apartment-hotel. *(Andrew Alpern)*

178 Mayfair House at 610 Park Avenue on the corner of 65th Street wraps around the little four-story private dwelling just south of it. *(Andrew Alpern)*

177

178

Columbia University Medical School

An early part of Columbia University was its College of Physicians and Surgeons. This distinguished medical school moved to the Washington Heights section of Manhattan in 1926, connected with the huge new Columbia Presbyterian Medical Center. Foreseeing the need for future expansion, it acquired additional property nearby as early as 1929. This land, lying between Haven Avenue and Riverside Drive, was originally a steep hillside of very rough terrain (Figure 179), but during the period following World War I, it was partially tamed, sufficient for a limited amount of residential development.

The school's physical plant grew at intervals as required by its expanding program and enrollment: a dormitory for single students was built, and in 1967 a large tract for a housing development for married students and faculty members was assembled. Together with the land purchased in 1929, this assemblage provided a frontage available for construction along Riverside Drive of almost three full blocks . . . except for a 50-foot-wide piece, 200 feet from the southern end of the property.

80 Haven Avenue The land which interrupted the Columbia assemblage was built almost solid with a six-story semi-fireproof apartment house which had been constructed by Saul Minskoff in 1926 to plans prepared by architect H. I. Feldman (Figure 180). Mr. Minskoff's nephews are still very active in New York's real estate industry. While most of the apartment houses along the west-

SEPT 2 1914

180

181

ern side of Haven Avenue had been built about 100 feet deep to the point where the land began to fall off sharply to Riverside Drive below, 80 Haven Avenue extended twice that distance, with massive structural supports at the western end that doubled the height of the rear elevation (Figure 181).

Since Columbia had not bought the 80 Haven Avenue property, the new Bard Haven housing project had to be designed accordingly. The architectural firm of Brown Guenther Battaglia Galvin planned a trio of apartment towers. The two northern ones sit on a podium base formed by a multilevel garage, while the base under the southern one contains apartments for the building's service personnel (Figure 182).

It initially appeared that each of the two sections of the project would require its own heating and air-conditioning system, but by a fortuitous circumstance, this was not necessary. In 1930, the Port of New York Authority acquired by condemnation a 10-foot parcel of land at the westerly end of the property on which 80 Haven Avenue had

been built. This land was taken for a widening of an access route to the then-new George Washington bridge, but only 5 feet of it was actually used. Columbia was able to acquire the remaining 5 feet and to use this ligature of earth as a point of connection between the two sections for the piping and conduits which obviated the need for duplicate mechanical systems.

180 From the front, 80 Haven Avenue looks much like other conventional apartment houses in the immediate neighborhood, if perhaps better maintained. It gives no indication of its curious rear elevation. *(Andrew Alpern)*

181 The rear elevation of 80 Haven Avenue shows clearly the effect of its site's topography. Although it encompasses only six stories, the land's drop-off between Haven Avenue and Riverside Drive doubles the structure's height. *(Andrew Alpern)*

182 The huge Bard Haven development built by Columbia University's medical school at 170th Street overlooking the Hudson River. Interrupting the project's continuity is a 200-foot-deep apartment house entered from Haven Avenue at its opposite end. *(Andrew Alpern)*

COLUMBIA UNIVERSITY MEDICAL SCHOOL 133

1134 Madison Avenue

183 An architectural rendering of the row of six townhouses and an apartment house that John H. Duncan designed for Madison Avenue at 84th Street in 1890. *(Courtesy of Christopher Gray, Office for Metropolitan History)*

184 The three remaining houses of the Duncan row. Sol Goldman's holdout is the last one; the single free-standing house was about to be razed at the time of the photograph. While the two lower floors of the avenue buildings have been altered for commercial uses, the corner house retains almost completely its original appearance. *(Andrew Alpern)*

On occasion, a holdout can have an unexpectedly beneficial and quite unplanned effect on its surroundings. The five-story onetime residence at 1134 Madison Avenue is a case in point. The refusal of its owner to sell to a developer assembling a large site for a new apartment tower led to the preservation of three important nineteenth-century townhouses.

In 1892, builder-developers James and Robert Lynd completed a speculative venture for which they had retained the services of John H. Duncan, the architect who designed Grant's Tomb. The two brothers constructed a row of six single-family residences and an apartment house on the west side of Madison Avenue north from 84th Street. The grouping had a visual coherence and a monumentality that was both unusual and impressive (Figure 183). The apartment house at the northern end of the row was 44 feet wide and contained two seven-room apartments on each floor. It was entered through a grand colonnaded porch surmounted by a pair of eagles, and had a marble-lined entrance lobby. The five midblock townhouses were 18 and 20 feet wide and were very finely built. By far the most impressive, however, was the 22-foot by 70-foot corner house. The entrance was a glass-enclosed porch, which still exists although the original stone stair has been replaced with a less imposing one. The building had an elaborately detailed interior that boasted a gas-log fireplace in the master bedroom and a billiard room in the basement, and the size of the house afforded space for twenty rooms.

When Madison Avenue was widened, the houses lost their high-stooped entrances, and later commercial develop-

183

ment dictated alterations to the ground and second floors for stores. Despite this, and despite some tasteless signs and the unfortunate outside painting of one of the houses, the entire row remained until 1980, when developer John Avlon began his truncation of the group with the demolition of number 1136 Madison Avenue.

Mr. Avlon had begun to assemble his building site in the mid-1970s and hoped to acquire the entire blockfront. Working his way south from 85th Street, he bought the Trans-Lux movie theater, the apartment house, and three of the former townhouses. He was blocked from going farther, however, when he could not come to terms with Sol Goldman, the owner of 1134. At this point—1977— the New York City Landmarks Preservation Commission was considering the designation of the Metropolitan Mu-

seum Historic District, an irregular area running from 78th Street to 86th Street and including most of each block between Fifth and Madison Avenues. In March of that year it held a hearing on the entire seven-building row that Mr. Duncan had designed. John Avlon pleaded with the commissioners to refrain from designating the portion of the Duncan row which he had acquired, since it would have a detrimental effect on his development plans if the buildings fell within the boundaries of the historic district.

The landmarks commission acquiesced to Mr. Avlon's pressures and drew the boundaries as he wished. In the process, the three southerly houses the Lynd brothers had built were saved from demolition, preserving at least a portion of Mr. Duncan's original design. Had Mr. Avlon been willing to pay Mr. Gold-

man's price for 1134, it is likely than the rest of the row would also have succumbed. Because of the holdout, however, the city gained more than just the holdout itself. A fine piece of New York's architectural history still exists, to the benefit of all New Yorkers—and ironically to the greatest benefit of the occupants of Mr. Avlon's new building. One of the best aspects of an urban environment is the intermixture of high- and low-rise buildings. While the retention of a single holdout of modest scale generally does visual damage to the cityscape, a consistent row complements a new development and enhances it. How fortuitous, then, for an individual holdout to have precipitated such a beneficial result (Figure 184).

184

919 Third Avenue

There is something about a venerable saloon that makes it a picturesque and almost lovable holdout . . . except perhaps to the real estate developer who wants to acquire it. P. J. Clarke's was a well-established institution long before Tishman Realty & Construction Company began to assemble the site for a new office building at 919 Third Avenue. It acquired notoriety in 1945 when it was supposedly used as a location for the filming of Ray Milland's barroom scenes in the movie "The Lost Weekend." Actually, the proximity of the Third Avenue elevated railway proved disruptive, and the final filming was accomplished in a studio reconstruction of the saloon built in California.

Mary G. Breslin built 915 Third Avenue on the corner of 55th Street in 1884. It had three floors of apartments above a ground floor saloon, which in 1904 was leased to Patrick Joseph Clarke, a young Irishman from county Leitrim.

P. J. Clarke's The pub was promptly christened P. J. Clarke's, and established a reputation as a home-away-

from-home for local politicians, newspaper reporters, writers, and others of that ilk. Mr. Clarke regularly renewed his lease, but shied away from suggestions that he buy the building.

Daniel and Matilda Lavezzo had an antique shop nearby, and in 1943 bought 915 as an investment. Paddy Clarke continued to run the saloon and occasionally to tend bar. When he died in 1948, his heirs tried to operate the bar themselves, but they quarreled. The following year they sold their interests to the Lavezzo family, and Danny Lavezzo, Jr. suddenly found himself cast into the role of a barkeeper. He ran the place skillfully, handling his patrons as deftly as his drinks. He expanded the kitchen and opened a large dining room in the back, and he hired Paddy's nephew Charles Clarke as manager. His business prospered, and with the dismantling of the old elevated structure in 1956, his profits grew more rapidly. With his extra capital he bought more property up the avenue from his saloon (Figure 185).

The Tishman interests had not yet completed their 909 Third Avenue of-

185

fice structure on the blockfront from 54th Street to 55th Street when they shifted operations one block to the north in a move to erect a similar building. They acquired most of the site they needed from 55th Street to 56th Street in 1967, but were stymied by Danny Lavezzo's insistence that P. J. Clarke's not succumb to "progress." Mr. Lavezzo held the trump card, since he also owned a midblock building that he wouldn't give up. Hard bargaining enabled the saloon owner to have his cake and eat it too. In exchange for $1.5 million, Mr. Lavezzo gave Mr. Tishman the deeds to both buildings, conditional on a ninety-nine-year lease for P. J. Clarke's.

In 1968, Mr. Tishman removed the upper two floors of 915 Third Avenue, and stabilized the structure of the saloon's old building. To accommodate the little watering hole, architects Skidmore Owings & Merrill placed the new office tower off-center on its site (Figure 186). At first, P. J. Clarke's building was completely freestanding on the newer building's plaza, but later a movie theater was constructed with its entrance filling in the space between the two structures From the sidewalk, however, P. J. Clarke's retains its cut-glass and wood-columned façade that preserves a small piece of the nineteenth-century ambience that once pervaded the entire length of Third Avenue (Figure 187).

185 The site of 919 Third Avenue in 1966. In the foreground is P. J. Clarke's at the corner of 55th Street. *(Lloyd Acker, courtesy of The New York Public Library)*

186 The Tishman interests placed the new 919 Third Avenue office structure off-center on its site to accommodate the P. J. Clarke saloon, whose owners insisted on the preservation of the venerable watering hole. *(Peter Roth, courtesy of The Durst Organization)*

187 P. J. Clarke's: A Third Avenue tradition since 1904, preserved as a very visible holdout. *(Andrew Alpern)*

186

187

43 Fifth Avenue

The shape of the built environment in New York is often an outgrowth of early farm lines and street patterns. Oddly angled building walls are likely to reflect property lines that parallel the boundaries of seventeenth- and eighteenth-century deed descriptions rather than the street patterns laid out early in the nineteenth century. Equally important to an understanding of existing holdouts is a knowledge of the early transactions involving the property around these holdouts. The language of those property transfers can tell how the land was used, and what restrictions were placed on its owners.

11 East 11th Street To determine why the diminutive holdout structure at 11 East 11th Street forced the rear apartment on each floor of 43 Fifth Avenue to assume an awkward configuration, it is necessary to investigate personalities and lifestyles of the mid-nineteenth century. During this period, the Greenwich Village area adjoining Fifth Avenue was developed with two important churches, and with complementary upper-middle-class one-family houses. The residents of many of these houses kept carriages and required separate buildings convenient to their homes in order to house their rigs and horses.

In 1850, James Donaldson had already built a substantial house at 43 Fifth Avenue on the corner of 11th Street. On the side street at the rear of his L-shaped lot, he erected a carriage house and stable. By placing this service structure well back from the street, Mr. Donaldson was able to create a front yard of sufficient size to permit the assembling of his equipage and the harnessing of the horses.

Besides the land on which his house and stable stood, Mr. Donaldson also owned the adjoining two lots on Fifth Avenue as well as the adjacent one on East 11th Street. Late in 1850, Mr. Donaldson sold his vacant land to George Wood, providing a strip of land 5 feet wide to connect the 11th Street property with the Fifth Avenue frontage. Mr. Wood needed the ligature so he could

188

189

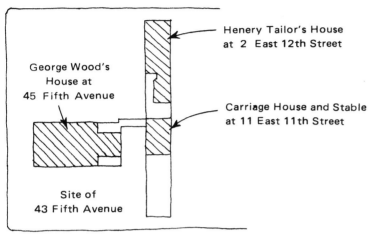

East 12th Street

Henery Tailor's House
at 2 East 12th Street

George Wood's
House at
45 Fifth Avenue

Carriage House and Stable
at 11 East 11th Street

Fifth Avenue

Site of
43 Fifth Avenue

190   East 11th Street

191

easily reach the stable he wanted to build on the side street from the house he intended to erect on the avenue.

Mr. Donaldson was concerned with appearances, however, and he didn't want his new neighbor to upstage his own newly built home. To assure this, he inserted a condition in his deed to Mr. Wood stipulating that Mr. Wood's new 48-foot-wide house not be any taller than Mr. Donaldson's corner house, and that the stable Mr. Wood intended to erect at 11 East 11th Street not be built any closer to the street than Mr. Donaldson's existing one at number 9 (Figure 188). Mr. Wood fulfilled the requirements of the indenture, and the two-story brick structure on 11th Street, which was later to become a holdout, was constructed with a front yard 65 feet deep (Figure 189). Later, after Mr. Wood died, his widow sold the stable, although she continued to live in the Fifth Avenue house.

In 1866, the stable built by Mr. Wood was bought by Henry A. Tailor, a lawyer. The same year Mr. Tailor bought the property around the corner at 2 East 12th Street. This was a fortuitous choice, since the rear lot line of the 12th Street property aligned perfectly with the back wall of the 11th Street stable (Figure 190). Mr. Tailor then built a large house of three stories and basement, plus a mansarded attic level. It was stylishly designed and appropriate for a rising young professional (Figure 191). Mr. Tailor was born in New York in 1833 and graduated from Columbia College

188 Lower Fifth Avenue in 1913. To the right is the house built in 1852 by George Wood, who also erected the holdout carriage house around the corner on 11th Street. Adjoining it is the much grander residence of Irad Hawley built the following year and still in existence. *(George F. Arata, courtesy of the Museum of the City of New York)*

189 The little mid-nineteenth-century one-time stable and carriage house at 11 East 11th Street blocked the developer of the adjoining luxury apartment house on Fifth Avenue at the beginning of the twentieth century. Its unusually deep front yard was the result of a deed restriction, and was originally used as a staging area for harnessing the horses. Behind the holdout is the rear of 2 East 12th Street, whose owner the stable once served. *(Gil Amiaga, courtesy of Stanley Lesser)*

190 Site plan of 11 East 11th Street.

191 The 1982 appearance of Henry A. Tailor's 1866 row house at 2 East 12th Street. The building's high stoop has been removed, and the attic and ground floors altered, but it retains the aura of spacious living that Mr. Tailor had sought. *(Andrew Alpern)*

in 1852, later studying law at universities in Germany. He was active in banking and railroad financing, and served as a vestryman to St. Bartholomew's Church. When he died in 1878, he left a life estate in his house and stable to his wife Sophia, with the property going to his children after her death.

In 1903, William E. Finn bought the former James Donaldson property including his house at 43 Fifth Avenue and his stable on 11th Street. Since the L-shaped lot was not ideally suited to the needs of the apartment house Mr. Finn hoped to erect, the developer attempted to purchase the land on which Mrs. Tailor's old stable stood. Perhaps feeling constrained by the terms of her husband's will, Sophia Tailor declined to sell. Forced to accept the limitations of the existing property lines, architect Henry Anderson planned an eleven-story apartment house whose grandly conceived beaux-arts façade concealed a floor plan comprising two ten-room suites per floor of which the rear unit was awkwardly elongated (Figure 192). Mr. Finn attempted to compensate for the poor floor plan by instructing his designer to embellish the building lavishly in the manner of the current fashion (Figure 193). Ornate or not, the apartments were slow to rent following their completion in 1905. The financial panic of 1907 found the building still

only partially occupied. Caught unprepared, Mr. Finn was not able to handle the building and its obligations, so he lost it in 1908 to a receivership.

Hemmed in by tall buildings on both sides, 11 East 11th Street continued to house Mrs. Tailor's carriage—and later her automobile—until her death in 1918. Sold by the estate, the 12th Street house was converted to apartments and the onetime stable was made over into a residence. The newly formed Conservative Synagogue of Fifth Avenue rented the building in 1959 and used it with minimal changes for religious services and meetings (Figure 194). In 1981 the congregation bought the little building and retained architect Edgar Tafel to plan alterations that would make the structure more responsive to the needs of the group.

Henry A. Tailor's house has been subdivided and the appearance of his carriage house obliterated. Each of the large apartments of 43 Fifth Avenue has been cut in two, and George Wood's spacious residence was demolished in 1925. Still existing, however, is the grandly Italianate mansion at 47 Fifth Avenue now housing the Salmagundi Club. Built in 1853 by Irad Hawley, it is the last remaining neighborhood vestige of the residential way of life that created the holdout at 11 East 11th Street (Figure 195).

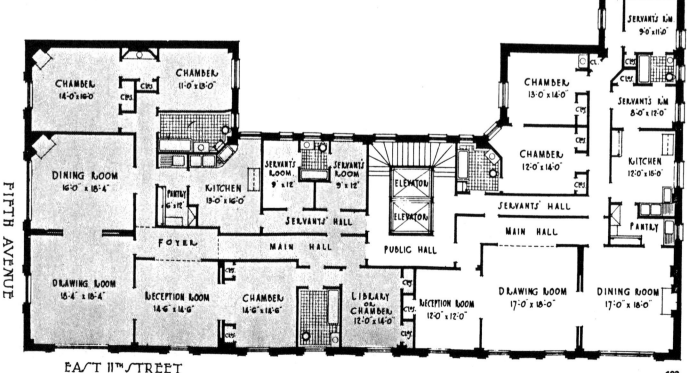

FIFTH AVENUE

EAST 11TH STREET

192

192 The floor plan of 43 Fifth Avenue as originally designed. The elongated configuration of the rear apartment was necessitated by the holdout on East 11th Street. These units have been subdivided in recent times.

193 As 43 Fifth Avenue appeared in 1982. The fire escape on the 11th Street side was added when the original ten-room suites were subdivided. *(Andrew Alpern)*

194 Set at the rear of its 25-foot-wide lot, 11 East 11th Street was given this appearance in the 1920s when it was converted for use as a residence. Since 1959, the building has served the needs of the Conservative Synagogue of Fifth Avenue. *(Gil Amiaga, courtesy of Stanley Lesser)*

195 The Salmagundi Club in the former Irad Hawley house at 47 Fifth Avenue. Houses such as this once lined lower Fifth Avenue, with their carriage houses on the nearby side streets. This one is all that remains of the living style which created the 11th Street holdout. *(Andrew Alpern)*

193

194

195

127 John Street

The office buildings constructed by the William Kaufman Organization have been known for their originality of conception and their whimsical design touches. To most passers-by, therefore, the huge digital clock at the corner of Water and John Streets would appear to have been a carefully planned part of the urbanistically vivacious design scheme of the office tower known by the address of 127 John Street—an appropriate foil for the brightly colored awnings, the playful sculptures, and the unusual street furniture provided by the building's developer.

Ironically, the real reason for the clock's existence is usually overlooked. Unobtrusively tucked in behind the 30-foot-high clock are two small buildings, joined at the ground floor by a restaurant. It was the refusal by the owner of one of these buildings to sell his property at a reasonable price that led to the concept of the clock that now charms and delights the people of the neighborhood.

During the 1960s, the longtime New York City developer William Kaufman acquired sixteen of the eighteen properties that comprised the block at Water and Fulton Streets on which he hoped to erect a new office tower. Mr. Kaufman anticipated providing general office space, as well as a new home for the New York Cocoa Exchange, but of course he wanted his new building to encompass the entire block. He didn't reckon on Robert Ardston, however.

Robert Ardston Mr. Ardston was a businessman, a sometimes politician, and a real estate investor who lived in Long Beach, Long Island. In 1954 he bought the four-story, 20-foot-wide building at 133 John Street from Martha Blank, giving back a mortgage on the property for part of the purchase price. Mr. Ardston later made some alterations to the building and removed the upper two stories.

Robert Ardston made other real estate investments, one of which proved very lucrative. He bought a very small corner property in the Wall Street area which the Lehman Brothers firm subsequently wanted to acquire in order to have what they considered a suitable site for a new building. Since they intended to construct an institutional building rather than a speculative one, they were willing to pay far more for Mr. Ardston's corner lot than what a customary financial analysis would have dictated. Consequently, Mr. Ardston received a reported $1 million as the holdout price for his little piece of property.

Having realized such an unusually high return on his original investment, Mr. Ardston may have thought that he'd be able to repeat the experience when he entered into negotiations to sell his John Street building to William Kaufman. Although the property could support a holdout price of perhaps $200,000, Mr. Ardston demanded the neat round figure of $1 million.

Number 135 was bought in 1959 by a Greek family. Emulating their next-door neighbor, they removed the top two floors of their five-story building, and then opened a restaurant on the ground floor level. A decade later, when considering the sale of their building to the Kaufman Organization, they asked Robert Ardston to negotiate on their behalf.

Apparently Mr. Ardston thought office building developers might be infinitely wealthy and able to pay virtually any price to assemble a construction site. Refusing to negotiate realistically, he exhausted the patience of William Kaufman, who passed the task of dealing with the recalcitrant holdout to his son Robert. Robert Kaufman was no more successful than his father in convincing Mr. Ardston that there was a relationship between the land price and the return that might be expected from the additional rentable area that could thereby be built. Robert soon gave up in favor of his brother Melvyn, who ultimately despaired of coming to acceptable terms with Mr. Ardston. Rather than pay an uneconomic price for the remaining two parcels, Mr. Kaufman cut a 4-foot by 41-foot notch out of his office tower, and a slightly larger piece out of the six-story base, and built around the pair of holdouts. To hide the raw exposed side of the Greek family's building, Mr. Kaufman devised the giant billboard-sized digital clock, thus turning what might have been a liability into a distinctive asset (Figure 196).

The Greeks did the best they could at that point by expanding their restaurant into Mr. Ardston's building. Both property owners are now stuck with their little buildings, the zoning laws severely limiting any future plans they might have for their land. The only benefit they have now from the Kaufman development is the increased restaurant patronage attributable to the occupants of 127 John Street, and the $200 per month rent Melvyn Kaufman pays for the privilege of stabilizing his giant clock face to the side of the little three-story structure at number 135.

196 The great bulk of 127 John Street wraps around the two little holdout buildings housing the John Street Restaurant. Melvyn Kaufman's whimsical giant digital clock serves as a screen to hide the bleak side wall of the holdout and provides a practical timekeeper for the neighborhood. *(Andrew Alpern)*

360 East 57th Street

197 A pseudo-holdout at Third Avenue and 57th Street. The little bank building on the corner appears to be a holdout against the newer apartment building behind it, but the developer owns the entire site. The apartment structure is built as high as is permitted by the zoning regulations, with no penalty for the bank building. While an office structure might want a complete corner plaza, a residential building does not require such an amenity. *(Andrew Alpern)*

West End Avenue

The West Side of Manhattan Island was much slower than the East Side in developing, primarily because of its lack of adequate public transportation. While omnibuses regularly ran up Second and Third Avenues as early as 1858, it was not until 1870 that anything more than the most desultory service was provided west of Central Park. The real impetus for land speculation and real estate development came in the late 1870s with the extended construction of the Ninth Avenue elevated railway. Recognizing this potential, in 1880 the city was successfully petitioned to change the name of Eleventh Avenue north of 70th Street to West End Avenue.

Since Central Park West and Riverside Drive were expected to provide sites for the city's finest mansions, land prices on those avenues soared. Speculators bought large segments of the available plottage and held on to them, awaiting the luxury boom that never came. Although Broadway was anticipated as a grand residential boulevard of slightly less lavish dwellings with West End Avenue accommodating local shops and services, it was Broadway which in fact developed as a commercial strip. Along with the side streets, West End Avenue became heavily built up with fine row houses, as well as with an occasional church. Two 1-block stretches of the avenue still remain essentially as they were originally built in the late nineteenth century. Both sides of West End Avenue from 76th to 77th Streets and again from 90th to 91st Streets illustrate what virtually the entire length of the avenue from 70th Street to 106th Street once looked like.

This "first growth" of West End Avenue buildings was generally more distinctive and individualistic than the earlier houses constructed farther south and on the East Side. The individualism of their owners was again demonstrated when large numbers of one-family dwellings were taken down to allow for a second generation of construction in the form of apartment houses that were built between the early years of the twentieth century and the 1920s. In a demonstration of defiance against the financial aspirations of developers and the housing aspirations of those who could not afford to live in row houses,

198 A holdout—232 West End Avenue—that had the inadvertently beneficial effect of permitting sidewall windows on the adjoining apartment buildings. *(Andrew Alpern)*

199A

199B

146   HOLDOUTS

a number of homeowners refused to sell. Attempting to cling to the smaller scaled residential ambience that was rapidly disappearing, these holdouts found themselves squeezed in beside huge overpowering apartment houses.

Generally, these little anachronisms break the otherwise-consistent streetwall and expose the blank brick sides of the adjoining structures that were never intended to be seen. Occasionally, however, advantage has been taken of adversity. Number 232 West End Avenue is an elegant and unusual limestone house midblock between 70th Street and 71st Street. The corner sites flanking the little house were being developed at the same time, and when the owner of the residence refused to sell to either of the builders, the two men realized that nothing of any significance would ever be erected on the land separating their two new apartment houses. Accordingly, they designed their buildings with windows along the side walls, giving good

light and air to what might otherwise have been dark courtyard rooms (Figure 198).

In most other cases of holdouts along West End Avenue, development was not so fortuitously timed, and the incongruities of the holdovers from the earlier development patterns intrude upon the newer buildings, rather than giving them any benefit (Figures 199 through 205).

199A & B West End Avenue as it originally looked along its entire length. Only the blocks from 90th to 91st Streets, and this one from 76th to 77th Streets, retain all their first-generation houses . . . and on both sides of the street. Where the other blocks generally reflect the second generation of residential construction, their consistency and coherence are occasionally marred by a holdout from the smaller-scaled past, breaking the rhythm and solidity of the streetwall. *(Andrew Alpern)*

200 Number 249 West End Avenue, seemingly compressed by its neighbors. *(Andrew Alpern)*

201 The building at 471 West End Avenue has been crudely converted to small apartments. It was originally a spacious one-family house—one of a group of six designed by McKim Mead & White and built by David H. King, Jr., in 1885–1886. *(Andrew Alpern)*

200

201

202

203

204

205

202 The building at 331 West End Avenue, incongruously nestled in between the two adjoining apartment houses. *(Andrew Alpern)*

203 The bow fronted holdout is at 788 West End Avenue. *(Andrew Alpern)*

204 The white holdout at the left, 605 West End Avenue, and 613 West End Avenue, practically hidden between the two large apartment buildings at the right. *(Andrew Alpern)*

205 Number 277 West 87th Street, at the corner of West End Avenue. *(Andrew Alpern)*

Park Avenue

The original naming of Park Avenue was akin to the naming of the country of Greenland—equal parts of wishful thinking and public relations. Appearing as Fourth Avenue on the new city street plan of 1811, the section from 34th to 36th Streets was renamed Park Avenue in 1860. By 1867 the appellation applied as far as 42nd Street, and this despite the open cut of the railroad tracks running from the car barns at 27th Street up the middle of the avenue. When the new Grand Central Depot was erected by Cornelius Vanderbilt in 1871 at 42nd Street, the Fourth Avenue tracks of the railroad north of the station were still at grade level, but the significantly increased traffic generated by the new terminal forced the sinking of the tracks into an open cut similar to the one south of 42nd Street.

With the trains below the level of the street, in 1888 Fourth Avenue became Park Avenue all the way up to Harlem. But with the smoke belching out from the coal-fired locomotives, the setting could hardly be described as parklike. It was not until the electrification of the trains running under the avenue and the completion of the new Grand Central Terminal building in 1913 that the open cut could be completely roofed over and the center planted malls constructed, thus giving Park Avenue a legitimate claim to its name.

Even with the trains running at grade or in the open cut, modest real estate development proceeded along Park Avenue. Small residential buildings, tenement houses, and a sprinkling of early apartment houses were built along the avenue, interspersed with factories and warehouses. But with the arrival of the landscaped center islands, the impetus was given to large-scale developers. Taking advantage of the avenue's extra width and the minipark down its middle, builders quickly erected a significant number of large, luxurious apartment houses. The convenient shopping provided just a block east or west, and the excellent public transportation afforded by the Lexington Ave-

206 The holdout at 985 Park Avenue exposes the bleak windowless sidewall of the adjoining building to the gaze of the passerby—a view that was never meant to be seen. The cost of maintaining the holdout has forced its owner to rent the ground floor to a grocery store, thus bringing commerce to what was intended to be a quiet residential boulevard. *(Andrew Alpern)*

207

208

209

210

nue subway and the elevated trains along Second and Third Avenues, assured a market for the high-rent accommodations being built.

With the greater profit potential enabling developers to pay higher prices for their building sites than was possible on the West Side, there were fewer holdouts to contend with. But human nature being what it is, a number of reluctant sellers emerged, to the detriment of the residents of the newer buildings. Part of the attraction of the expensive apartment houses was a direct outgrowth of their cost; the price one had to pay to live on Park Avenue excluded those considered to be less desirable neighbors. Except, of course, in the case of the holdouts. While today's astronomical housing prices have made even the tenement house apartments on the avenue accessible to only the very rich, in

the period before World War II, flats in the earlier buildings could be rented by those thought to be inferior by the residents of the grander and newer buildings. This, together with the ground floor commercial shops in some of the holdout buildings, detracted from the otherwise exclusive and rarified atmosphere carefully cultivated by developers and residents alike.

Aside from the economic undesirability of the holdouts on Park Avenue, these survivor buildings do architectural damage to the streetscape as well. The finest and most elegant avenues in Europe are broad boulevards with consistent streetwalls of buildings of uniform height. Park Avenue approaches this ideal, except where the little holdout buildings intrude to breach the continuity and consistency of the fifteen-story cornice lines (Figures 206 through 211).

211

207 A nineteenth-century relic—957 Park Avenue—at the corner of 82nd Street destroys the economic and architectural consistency of the avenue, but it is the tiny two-story art gallery at 949 Park Avenue that most aggressively flaunts its status as a holdout. *(Andrew Alpern)*

208 While 1055 Park Avenue on the corner of 87th Street parallels the visual damage of the holdout of 957 five blocks south, it was a developer rather than a holdout that broke the façade continuity in the middle of the block. Instead of maintaining the building line, the developer of 1045 Park Avenue interrupted it with a gate for deliveries and service access. *(Andrew Alpern)*

209 Cheaply constructed tenements from the 1880s were the speculator's answer to New York's burgeoning population. Although much urban renewal effort has been expended at replacing them, one remains at 1067 Park Avenue. Its intrusion on the otherwise-entrenched elegance is lessened perhaps by the inappropriate and inconsistent architecture of its newest neighbor at number 1065 to the south. *(Andrew Alpern)*

210 The two little antiquated holdout buildings at 1108 and 1110 Park Avenue expose the unadorned sidewall of the adjacent luxury apartment house at 1100 Park, and destroy the continuity of what would otherwise be a grand residential avenue. *(Andrew Alpern)*

211 While 407 Park Avenue appears to be a holdout not unlike others on the avenue, in fact it was held as a light protector by the developer of the limestone-faced apartment building at number 417 to the north. Since his architect placed essential windows on the sidewall of the larger structure, the developer purchased the little building to ensure that no newer building would ever be erected to block the windows of his apartment investment. *(Andrew Alpern)*

Fifth
Avenue

212A & B There is a curious similarity between these two holdout buildings at 1014 and 1033 Fifth Avenue. The one opposite the Metropolitan Museum of Art was built as a residence in 1906 and is now tenanted by Goethe House, a German-American cultural center. It is 25 feet wide—a standard New York City building lot. The other building, two blocks farther north, is only 5 feet narrower yet it appears to be far more compressed. It was constructed in 1870 for Harriet Trask and altered to its present form for George C. Smith in 1912. Like 1014, 1033 was built as a one-family residence; remarkably it is still occupied as such. (*Lloyd Acker, courtesy of The New York Public Library [left], and Andrew Alpern [right]*)

212A

212B

120 Wall Street

Located at 120 Wall Street is a thirty-three-story office building containing nearly half a million square feet of rentable space. Completely filling the zoning envelope, it was built as densely on its plot as the laws then allowed (Figure 213). Clearly, its developers wanted to make maximum use of the site, yet there is a narrow slot running up the building's north façade, diminishing the size of each floor by 180 square feet, and the rental income in proportion (Figure 214). The slot is there because there is a piece of land 9 feet wide and 20 feet deep in the Pine Street frontage of the property on which nothing was built. When the architectural firm of Buchman & Kahn designed 120 Wall Street in 1929, instructions were given that no portion of the building was to rest on that small plot of land, nor was the structure to extend over it (Figure 215). No land map of New York has ever shown a building on that spot, and the land doesn't even appear in the tax records of the city. To find an unused piece of land in a part of Manhattan that has been so intensely and repeatedly developed is curious. Even more curious is the reason for it, and to trace this apparently nameless holdout it is necessary to go back to the eighteenth century when New York was ruled by King George III.

Human beings are by nature clustering creatures; they want to be where the action is perceived to be. This has been evident during the past decade in the intense east-midtown commercial development that has ignored the many underutilized and readily available sites further west and south. And it was evident 250 years ago when all of New York was clustered at the southern end of Manhattan Island.

The original shoreline along the East River approximated the line of today's Water Street. When space in the colonial town became tight, instead of expanding to the north as logic would have dictated, eighteenth-century New Yorkers chose to remain close-in by creating new land along the riverfronts at both sides of the island. Before the midcentury point had been reached, the East River's edge had been moved eastward to Front Street by the creation of filled land.

William William Brownjohn was a
Brownjohn druggist with a flourishing business on Hanover Square. He owned property on Front Street along a strip then known as Hunter's Key [Quay] or Rotten Row (more probably borrowed from the fashionable London promenade rather than being descriptive). In 1750 he petitioned the city government for the right to purchase from the mu-

nicipality the water lot in front of his property so he might create new filled land further out into the East River. Unanswered, he repeated his petition in 1754 and then again in 1765. When he filed papers again in 1766, the Common Council termed his request "insolent and impertinent," and ordered that it be "thrown under the table." A persistent man, Mr. Brownjohn kept up his pressure on the council, and in 1770 his petition was granted, although it was not until 1772 that he was finally given a deed to the water lot he had worked so long to obtain.

Mr. Brownjohn's water grant was 41 feet wide and extended into the river toward an imaginary line which has since become South Street. As a condition of the grant, within five years Brownjohn was required to widen Front Street by 5 feet along his property line, to extend King Street (now called Pine Street) out into the river, to construct a new wharf at the line of the new waterfront, and of course to fill in his new land. Before Mr. Brownjohn had done these things, however, the American colonies de-
The clared their independence
Revolution from King George and war brought all thought of construction work to a halt. During most of the period of the fighting, the British occupied the city, not leaving until November of 1783. New York began to pick up the pieces at that point and to rebuild and expand the war-ravaged city, but William Brownjohn died early in 1784 before he could enjoy the fruits of the country's newly minted freedom.

The wealthy druggist left a substantial estate in trust for the benefit of his wife Mary during her lifetime, with his children inheriting at her death. She died, and in 1793 his executors sold the property defined by the water grant to Robert Bruce, whose son William inherited the property at his father's death in 1796. William Bruce subdivided the property, creating among others, two lots fronting on South Street, each about 21 feet wide and about 70 feet deep. Reflecting the burgeoning economy's need for commercial buildings along the waterfront to service the increasing trans-Atlantic ship trade, Bruce erected buildings on the two lots, the one at the corner having a small backyard, with the other extending the full depth of the lot.

213 A 1930 photograph of 120 Wall Street before any tenants had moved in. This view shows the Wall Street and South Street façades; the Pine Street side with its holdout is hidden from sight. *(Courtesy of Donald Weill)*

Privy Rights   In 1804, Mr. Bruce sold the inner lot, known as 67 South Street, to Amasa Jackson for $5250. Recognizing that Mr. Jackson's newly acquired building completely covered his lot, Mr. Bruce included in the deed the "privilege of the necessary" on the adjoining lot. In simple terms, Mr. Bruce gave Mr. Jackson the right to use the privy in his own backyard.

William Bruce retained 68 South Street—the building at the corner of Pine Street—but was forced to relinquish it in 1812 to satisfy a debt to the New York Firemen Insurance Company. The insurance company in turn sold the property in 1814 to John Griswold, but did so in a manner which created a totally intractable holdout 115 years later. The company recognized that its own ownership of 68 South Street's backyard was subject to "the privilege of the necessary" granted to Amasa Jackson ten years **The Privy Is Not Sold** earlier. Instead of deeding to Mr. Griswold the entire property subject to that easement, however, they gave to Mr. Griswold only the building and the land under it, together with the right to use the existing outhouse in the backyard. Whether or not they intended to do so, the officers of the insurance company retained ownership of that 9-foot by 20-foot yard by the wording of their deed.

New York Firemen Insurance Company had been founded in 1810 under a capitalization of $500,000, with Wil-

liam Lovett serving as president and William McNeil as secretary. By 1822, its capital had dropped to $200,000 and its name changed to Hope Marine Insurance Company. John Whetten had become president, but William McNeil remained secretary. The renamed com- **The Privy Owner Vanishes** pany was able to improve its financial position to $300,000, but in 1826 it ceased doing business. All records of the firm and its stockholders disappeared.

With the advent of indoor plumbing, the backyard privy was removed, but nothing was ever built on the site, since no one could clear the title to the little plot of land.

A group called Lawyers Realty Company assembled the 120 Wall Street site around 1917, and in 1922 sold the assemblage to the American Sugar Refining Company. For the first time since 1812, the deed description *included* the outhouse holdout site. In 1929, the sugar company transferred the property to Henry Greenberg and David Malzman (as Greenmal Holding Company) using the same inclusive property description. The new owners ordered a title search before proceeding, and discovered that they didn't own all that they thought they did. Although their deed gave them the entire site, title couldn't be insured for **The Vacant Privy Site** the ancient yard, so they placed prudence at the forefront and refrained from building on the holdout land. They may have in-

tended to complete their building after having established "adverse possession" of the ownerless land for the statutory period since their architects planned the structure so it could be readily "filled in" at a later date. They never had an opportunity to do so, however, since they lost the building in 1933 to foreclosure by the holder of the mortgage.

Recently 120 Wall Street has been renovated and refurbished by its new owner Larry Silverstein, who had accepted the missing piece of the Pine Street façade as merely one more eccentricity in a half-century old building. Rejuvenated, it is likely to remain for a long time as a substantial and prestigious office building, perhaps the only one ever to encounter an outhouse as a holdout.

214 The impossibility of building on the little holdout plot resulted in this strange slot in the north facade of 120 Wall Street. *(Andrew Alpern)*

215 A typical floor plan of 120 Wall Street clearly showing the effect of the holdout.

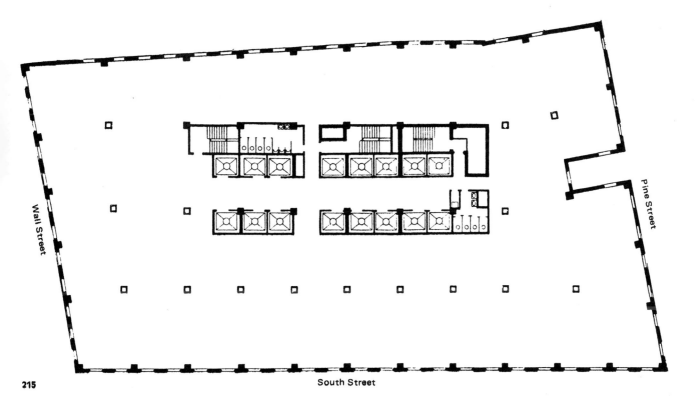

215

Wall Street

Pine Street

South Street

Morgan Guaranty

A stubborn holdout who refuses to deal realistically with a developer and who insists on an absurdly high buy-out price may very well be left holding the bag when the uneconomic cost of acquiring the holdout dooms the entire development. This sort of scenario is particularly regrettable when the holdout owner stands to benefit from the development in ways that go beyond this selling price of the holdout property.

New York City In 1980, this precise course of events was played out in lower Manhattan with the City of New York itself taking the role of the intractable holdout.

The developer was the Morgan Guaranty Trust Company of New York, whose headquarters building is at the corner of Broad Street and Exchange Place in the heart of Manhattan's financial district. With additional space scattered among half a dozen other buildings in lower Manhattan, Morgan Guaranty needed to consolidate its operations and hoped to accomplish this by assembling a site across Exchange Place from its headquarters and erecting a giant new office building on the property. As its agent, it retained James Austrian, a partner in the international real estate consulting firm of Jones Lang Wootton.

The desired site comprised six existing high-rise structures (Figure 216), with the greatest attention focused on three of them. The largest was controlled by veteran real estate operator Harry Helmsley who also owned the Empire State Building; another was owned by investor Joseph Wohl; the third was in the hands of Sol Goldman, who had once owned the Chrysler Building. It took only two weeks for Mr. Austrian to contract for the Wohl building for $6.8 million. The Helmsley property acquisition was more complex, but a few months of negotiating resulted in an agreement at a figure of $19 million.

The negotiations with Mr. Goldman were conducted entirely over the telephone and concluded with an agreement on a sales price of $2.7 million, subject to Mr. Goldman's paying a bill for back taxes of $1.7 million. The fly in the ointment was an action by the city seizing the building for nonpayment of the tax bill. While under ordinary circumstances the city would have relinquished its newly acquired title in exchange for the taxes, in this case the city refused to give back the property. This forced Mr. Austrian and Morgan Guaranty to approach the city with their project in an effort to buy the building directly.

Mr. Austrian assumed that the city would be happy to sell, since the Morgan Guaranty project would give the city more than $13 million a year in annual taxes after its completion, compared to a yield from the three existing buildings of hardly more than $1 million. He offered $2 million, hoping to improve on the price Mr. Goldman had been willing to accept, and was taken aback when the city demanded $17 million. The Goldman price had equated to $136 per square foot; top sales prices at the time for comparable land did not exceed $150 per foot; the city wanted $850! After three months of discussions during which the city's representatives moved only very slightly on their price, Morgan Guaranty gave up and declared the development dead. The city was left with a boarded-up derelict building, a huge unpaid tax bill, and a spectacularly lost opportunity. Three years later, the city was finally able to auction off the parcel . . . but too late to save the bank project that could have brought so much benefit to the municipal interests. *Sic transit gloria civitas.*

216 This is the group of buildings at Broad Street and Exchange Place that could have been the site of a huge institutional office building had it not been for the overreaching pricing and the shortsightedness of the City of New York. *(Peter B. Kaplan and* Fortune *magazine)*

Brevoort Estate

Even before the name of Nieuw Amsterdam was permanently changed to New York in 1664, the Brevoort family had been involved with the development of the city. A succession of Brevoorts built businesses and bought land on Manhattan Island, doing both with a vigor and tenacity that manifested itself later in a refusal to yield private land to public purposes—a holdout against the ultimate developer . . . the city itself.

An early Brevoort established a family seat in the vicinity of what is now Broadway and 11th Street. The house he built was served by the Bowery road (now Fourth Avenue), which continued on further north as the Eastern Post Road. An early Hendrick Brevoort (there were several of that name in the family) has been said to have been one of the first holdouts against the progress of the city toward the northern end of Manhattan Island. According to tradition, this old Dutch burgher had a favorite tree behind his house whose continued existence was threatened by the plans of the city to extend the Middle Road northward through his property. Supposedly standing off the surveyors with his gun, he forced the course of the road extension to bend westerly as it passed his estate. Another story has it that the bend in what by then was called Broadway was caused by a miscalculation on the part of the board of commissioners who laid out the city streets in 1809. But whether it was Mr. Brevoort's obstinacy or the commissioners' lack of care, Broadway takes a bend at 10th Street on its way north, bringing it parallel to Fourth Avenue, the Bowery's extension (Figure 217).

Better documented are the holdout tactics of the later Henry Brevoort. His story began with the commissioners' map of city streets, which preserved the strip of land between Broadway and the Bowery from 10th Street to 16th Street, calling it Union Place. Mr. Brevoort's ancient homestead lay within Union Place, which was unencumbered by cross streets.

In 1815, it was decided that Union Place inhibited traffic across the island, and a legislative act was passed reducing it in size to what is now Union Square, and calling for the opening of 11th, 12th,

217 North on Broadway from 9th Street. The excellent view of Grace Church is made possible by the bend Broadway takes at 10th Street. The change in direction of the great highway may have been due to the refusal of an early Hendrick Brevoort to permit Broadway to be cut through his land in a manner that would require the removal of his favorite tree. *(Andrew Alpern)*

218 Looking west along 11th Street. The street stops at Fourth Avenue, resuming its course on the other side of Broadway. The discontinuity is a direct result of holdout Henry Brevoort's resistence to the efforts of the city fathers to cut the street through in 1836 and again in 1849. *(Andrew Alpern)*

219 The Brevoort land and its surrounding streets.

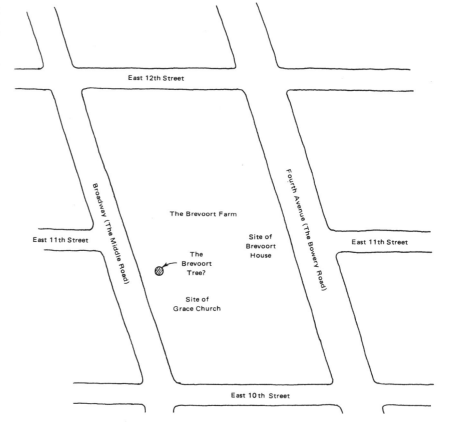

East 12th Street

East 11th Street

Broadway (The Middle Road)

Fourth Avenue (The Bowery Road)

The Brevoort Farm

Site of
Brevoort
House

East 11th Street

The
Brevoort
Tree?

Site of
Grace Church

East 10th Street

13th, and 14th Streets to connect Broadway and the Bowery. The three northerly streets were opened without difficulty, but in 1836 when an attempt was made to cut through 11th Street, a vigorous protest was lodged by Henry Brevoort, whose large old house was directly in the path of the proposed new street. Mr. Brevoort's relentless pressure tactics, coupled with the depressed state of the city's economy at the time, were sufficient to have the street work delayed indefinitely.

Thinking that the city's plans for 11th Street had been permanently tabled, Mr. Brevoort sold much of his land in 1843 to the congregation of Grace Church. The church elders too assumed that the matter had been laid to rest, and they constructed a grand edifice to the designs of Mr. Brevoort's nephew, James Renwick, Jr., completing it in 1846. The city's plans were not dead, however, and an attempt was again made to open 11th Street for the convenience of pedestrians and conveyances.

In its efforts to garner support for opening the street, the city solicited letters of approval for its actions from prominent local citizens, including the venerable Peter G. Stuyvesant. Equally stubborn in opposing the opening was old Henry Brevoort, backed by the considerable political and social power of the members of Grace Church. While the church stood to lose the potential for northerly expansion if the street were to be opened, and thus had a strong interest in opposing the city, Mr. Brevoort's motives were not so clear. He had already sold most of his land for development, and his family manse had long since been demolished. Perhaps the family tradition for holding out was too ingrained in him to permit him to quit, so he persisted. His tenacity paid off, and in 1849, the city planners gave up their efforts and altered the official street map to close the stretch of 11th Street which had never actually been opened in the first place (Figures 218 and 219).

2054 Anthony Avenue, The Bronx

The Grand Boulevard and Concourse, popularly known as the Grand Concourse, was conceived in 1890 by Louis Aloys Risse, an engineer in the employ of the city. Construction of this important Bronx avenue was begun in 1902 and the work was completed in 1909. Development of the area in the vicinity of the new Concourse paralleled its planning and construction and included a long row of modest one-family frame houses on Anthony Avenue, north of Burnside Avenue and one block to the east of the Grand Concourse.

These dwellings were simple and small—generally about 17½ feet to 25 feet wide. They had bay windows and diminutive front porches, their most distinguishing feature being their octagonal roof turrets. They were erected for families of moderate means who were seeking an escape to the expanses of the Bronx from the crowded conditions and high rents of Manhattan, and they served

that purpose well until the 1930s (Figure 220).

During the Great Depression, land values plummeted. Since building materials and labor were relatively cheap, those with foresight and ready cash bought up much of the Bronx's stock of one-family homes in order to tear them down and build apartment houses. One developer assembled the site from 2056 to 2064 Anthony Avenue and erected a six-story apartment house in a minimally art deco style. Just before World War II, another developer assembled a comparable site further south on the street, but was unable to buy number 2054 from Isaac Sear, who had bought the house in 1926 after having rented it from Marie O'Connor for a number of years. Perhaps seeking to retain the scale and charm of the Queen Anne styling of the little house, Sear wouldn't budge (Figure 221).

The house is still there, but much like

220 Anthony Avenue, south of East 180th Street in the Bronx. This is what remains of the north end of the holdout's brothers and sisters. What once had been a uniform row of charmingly simple clapboard frame houses has been degraded by the alteration of the octagonal turrets and the tasteless application of imitation stonework, aluminum siding, and metal awnings. *(Andrew Alpern)*

221 The building at 2054 Anthony Avenue in the Bronx. Once part of a seventeen-house row of two-story Queen Anne style residences built at the beginning of the century, it seems overwhelmed by the apartment houses that now flank it. *(Gil Amiaga)*

220

221

the little house in the *Punch* cartoon or the one sculpted by Gifford Myers (Figures 222 and 223), what Mr. Sear sought to retain was destroyed by the very same forces that he had thought were successfully repulsed. A pyrrhic victory, to say the least.

"No, I refused to be bought out; you see, I was fond of the place and its surroundings."

222 Art imitates life. A cartoon that appeared in an English humor magazine in 1932 paralleling the little frame holdout on Anthony Avenue. *(Fougasse, courtesy of* Punch *and Rothco)*

223 "Hold Out," a 6-inch-square wall-mounted ceramic sculpture created in 1980 by Gifford Chandler Myers. The sculptor describes it as representing "a small family residence crowded between two high rises and owned by someone to whom a home is still a home . . . no matter how inflated the value of the property has become." *(Gifford Chandler Myers)*

223

Joann B. Erickson, courtesy of National Graphic Art Society

Index